HE HEARD HANNAH

By Lynnette Kraft
with Courtney Becker

HE HEARD HANNAH

For information, address Comfort Publishing, 296 Church St. N., Concord, NC 28025. The views expressed in this book are not necessarily those of the publisher.

Copyright ©2012 by Lynnette Kraft
Library of Congress Control Number:

First printing

Book cover design
by Reed Karriker

ISBN: 978-1-936695-45-4
Published by Comfort Publishing, LLC
www.comfortpublishing.com

Printed in the United States of America

ENDORSEMENTS

"This is a powerful story of transformation. If you allow yourself to listen closely it is likely you will hear what 911 Dispatcher Courtney Becker heard. Not just the name of a child, but the very whisper of God calling, *Come to me, you who are broken and weary, and I will give you rest.*"

—*Chris Green, President of Responder Life*

"I was pulled into this awesome story ... this is one of the best books I have ever read ... Glory to God! He writes awesome stories, doesn't He? This is definitely one of them."

— *Gracia Burnham, author, of New York Times Best Seller*
In the Presence of My Enemies

"Every so often, God pulls the curtain aside and rewards your faith with evidence. *He Heard Hannah* is a view through the veil."

— *Serena Woods, bloggist and author of* Grace is For Sinners

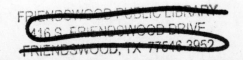

DEDICATION

I dedicate this book to my daughter, Anna Gabrielle Kraft. Without her, this story simply wouldn't exist ...

Precious daughter, I fell deeply in love with you as you lived.

Your life, changed mine forever.

Your death awakened a desire in me ... a desire to love people openly, willingly and sincerely, just as you did. My heart was a bud that came into full bloom.

Your life left an imprint on the hearts of every person who knew you and loved you, and every person who knew you ... loved you.

Your death opened up an opportunity for new life in Jesus Christ for Courtney, and I pray others will come to know Him through this story as well.

Your life will never be forgotten Anna. You *are* simply unforgettable.

Your death will never be forgotten. It changed a man's eternal destiny!

Anna, your momma, your daddy, Jared, Abigail, Cecily, Silas, Jonas and Harrison are all greatly anticipating the day we will live with you for eternity. You are still very much a part of our family. What a gift to know we will live together again ... forever.

Anna Gabrielle, I love you.

(Jesus, thank you for the gift of Anna's life.)

Love,
Your Momma

P.S. Can you hear me smile?

FOREWORD

By Clarke T. Cayton
Vice President of Content, Responder Life

Have you ever found yourself living in two different worlds at the same time? I certainly have. When I was 19, I entered the worlds of both Bible College (affectionately known as "The Bubble") & professional EMS. I would spend all week in classes learning about Old Testament History, Pauline Literature, and Biblical Hermeneutics, only to leave campus every weekend for two 12 hour shifts on an ambulance, running calls and witnessing the world at its worst. It didn't take long for me to notice that I was asking very different questions than my peers in class. The "911 World" that I was living in exposed me to homicides, suicides, overdoses, and car crashes. This all presented a real challenge for me as I sought to understand, "Where is God in all of this"?

For every First Responder, there is no greater emotional challenge than working a pediatric code (a child in cardiac arrest). Within every one of us, there is an internal voice that screams, "This is NOT how it is supposed to be!" I remember my first call involving the death of a child. I remember how numb I felt afterwards. Even now writing this, I feel my heart sink into my gut as my mind floods with the details of that night. Imagine experiencing that on a Sunday night and then the next morning sitting through a Systematic Theology class talking about superficial hypotheticals. I began to have some real questions! Yet, no one on campus seemed to understand…

Only those who have experienced this kind of trauma first hand, have a perspective of how deeply the soul aches – it's far beneath the glossy veneer of what society calls, "normal life".

I am grateful that my friends, Lynnette Kraft and 911 Dispatcher Courtney Becker, have chosen to share their incredible story with the world. I will tell you that what you are about to read is raw and written from the brokenness of their own hearts. The questions they ask of God, independently of one another, are real and authentic. They are the voices of thousands of families and First Responders who continually cry out, "Where is God in all of this?"

There is a fundamental certainty that occurs in the midst of every tragedy, when we are forced to confront a new reality that none of us can ever fully be prepared to realize. Our worldview is left shattered and life no longer makes sense. It leaves us in a desperate scramble for answers and for truth. For too many people, scenarios like this are beyond any personal reconciliation and they can often lead down a lifelong path of disillusionment, depression and despair. For those who turn their ear to God and hear His words of eternal life, peace and dare I say even JOY, can be a known reality once more.

In this story, you will encounter a family whose faith in the midst of tragedy defies the logic of the world. How could they trust God through such tremendous heartache and grief? Could God actually be right in the middle of all of their tragedy?

If you've ever found yourself disheartened and questioning, as I have, then this book will surely speak to you. Give God the chance to tell his story through the lives of people who have been there when life is at its darkest. We all find ourselves on a journey. For some, it is a matter of keeping faith, for others, it's a matter of finding it.

Now with great privilege, I invite you to witness the life-story fusion of Lynnette, a broken-believer longing for her faith to rescue her — and Courtney, a broken-rescuer longing for the faith to believe.

INTRODUCTION

Jeremiah 33:3 says, "Call unto me and I will answer thee and show thee great and mighty things, which thou knowest not." I've always looked at "great and mighty things" as God's surprises for me, and this story is about one of those surprises. It wasn't just for me and my family, though, it was also for Courtney and his family. When God revealed that work to us, we all stood amazed!

I'm telling Courtney's and my story side by side because that's how you'll discover the beauty of God's magnificent plan. Each odd-numbered chapter is my story, and each even-numbered chapter is Courtney's.

We were strangers before these events took place. We know it was destiny that allowed our families to meet along what started as separate paths. Our lives intersected in an amazing and unbelievable way that only God could have directed. It was nothing short of a miracle that God created something so perfect out of something so painful.

Lynnette

CHAPTER 1

In the middle of summer, when the temperature is topping out at over 100 degrees and the only way to stay cool is to sit on an air conditioner vent and drink lemonade, most full-term pregnant women would be doing anything and everything to bring on labor. Extreme heat and an extra 35 pounds of baby weight make for a miserable existence. I *was* that full-term pregnant woman, and it was the middle of a very hot and humid summer, but I wasn't walking the malls or eating spicy foods to induce labor. I knew the days following Anna's birth would be like war for her and for us, and I wasn't ever going to be prepared to face those days. I knew the string of events that was destined to take place would have to begin by nature, not by choice.

Anna's heart wasn't "normal" and would require several surgeries and a lot of care to function in a way that would sustain her life. We were somewhat terrified as we anticipated her birth and especially our future, but we were also grateful for the hope her doctor had given us. We were choosing to trust God in our fear and we knew He would carry us through the unpredictable

1

days ahead.

Anna was our sixth child and the third to be diagnosed with a congenital defect (each one entirely different from the other). She wouldn't meet her two brothers, Samuel and Josiah, on this side of Heaven, but she had three excited siblings awaiting her arrival — her brother Jared and her sisters, Abigail and Cecily.

I wish I could say that the death of my baby boys had increased my faith to the point that I could move mountains with it. The simple truth was that I trusted God and knew He was faithful, but I knew more than ever how weak and incapable I was. I didn't want to go through the horrible pain of watching my baby die, but even more than that, I was scared to death to love and care for a child that would be sick. I'd journeyed down a frightening path twice that lead to the death of my precious babies and had found victory, but this unfamiliar path that was before me somehow seemed even more terrifying. I was so afraid I'd be lost and confused traveling upon it. What if I wasn't capable of raising a sick child? What if death came after I'd loved my daughter for many years? I found myself wishing it could just end quickly. I couldn't foresee the blessings ahead. Fear threatened to consume me.

If I didn't begin my morning in God's word, allowing it to enrich my spirit, by the end of the day I was a crumpled mess. The benefit of past trials was that I knew where to run and I was confident that the one I was running to would faithfully be there. Still … I constantly fought the temptation to flee. I wanted to be spared every bit of pain. I had no plans to end the life of my child, but at times I wished God would, so I could heal and move on.

On the other hand, my daughter had a fighting chance at life, and I wanted to fight with her and for her. I wasn't sure what the road ahead looked like and it was the not knowing that made the waiting such torture. I desperately wanted to get back to the boring, mundane things in life. I craved routine and simplicity and hated that my mind was always preoccupied with the distressing world of the unknown. I wanted to trust God. I wanted to be strong for my daughter. I wanted Anna in my arms forever. Yet, I wanted to quit. It was a battle between my weak flesh and my hopeful spirit.

Not uncommon for me, contractions had started, increased in intensity, become closer together and then piddled out for several days. However, on July 25, 1998, after a few visits to my midwife, Kathy (who was also a good friend), I discovered I was making progress. It was likely I would give birth sometime that day. I stayed home as long as I could. I was in no hurry to make my way to the hospital because I knew that, once I was admitted, I would be forced to come to terms with the reality that my daughter might not survive. At least in my womb she was safe. I could hold her close and meet her needs as long as she remained inside of me. I knew that would change once the cord was cut. At that point she would be transferred from the safety of my womb to the NICU. There would be doctors who would understand her better than her own mother. They would be the ones to sustain her life outside the womb. I wanted to be able to care for her every need, but her problems were beyond my understanding. I couldn't use natural remedies to fix them as I did with so many other things. I desperately hoped that the excruciating pain of labor would reward me with a baby I could return home with.

*****

We finally made our way to the hospital at about 8:00 pm. I knew it was time to go when Kathy said my cervix was dilated to six centimeters. By the time we got to the hospital, I was seven centimeters dilated. Things progressed quickly and just before midnight on July 25, 1998, I was holding my baby girl — Anna Gabrielle. To say I enjoyed the birth would be an exaggeration; however, in comparison to my other deliveries, it was actually fairly easy. I rejoiced as I held my plump, slightly purple baby. She had a thick mass of wavy black hair that reminded me of Abigail. Anna was beautiful, and I felt what every new mother feels — instant, enveloping love.

I hemorrhaged a bit after Anna's birth, and that's what kept me from being able to travel with her to Kansas City. Anna's daddy — my husband, Kyle — would be the one to accompany her on the private flight. Her personal flight crew was there to meet her every need until she was placed in the care of the doctors and nurses at Children's Mercy Hospital.

After I was discharged from the hospital, I went home to pack our bags so the rest of us could be with Kyle and Anna. I didn't know how long we'd be there, but I did know that Anna would have her first heart surgery while we were in Kansas City. I was tired and wished I could just settle in bed with my baby next to me. I wanted to be cared for as a new mother normally would be. Instead, I was called to duty. The battle had officially begun. I had been terrified of entering the world of unknowns, but somehow being in the midst of it gave me renewed courage.

I didn't want to be away from my other children, so my parents came along to help with them. Dad drove separately so we would have two cars while there, and Mom drove the kids and me later that day. Although it wasn't a long drive, it seemed to take forever. I wasn't feeling well. We were all tired and emotionally spent. By the time I was able to be with Anna again, it had been nearly 24 hours. I'd had her with me for nine months and those hours being apart created a deep longing. My body craved hers, and I knew her body was craving mine as well. I was certain our hearts were both feeling the pains of separation.

When we arrived at the hospital the next morning, we were briefed on Anna's current condition and were given more bad news. We had been told while I was still carrying her that her heart issues were part of a condition called Heterotaxy Syndrome. This is a disorder that results in certain organs forming on the opposite side of the body. It's often associated with spleen malformations as well. The less serious form is called Polysplenia, meaning the spleen is in many little pieces, but still slightly functional. Asplenia is the complete absence of a spleen. We were initially told that Anna had Polysplenia, but after performing a sonogram, they changed their diagnosis. Anna had no spleen at all. This meant that she would be more susceptible to infection — new information that caused more anxiety for me.

While doing a sonogram of Anna's heart and organs, the doctor casually pointed out her uterus. Seeing that in my daughter made me wonder about her future. I found myself hoping that womb would carry a child someday. With my other living children, I dreamed about what they might become, when they would marry and how many children they might have. I wanted to dream the same things for Anna, and I hoped that she'd have all of the same opportunities my other children would have. I was too afraid to ask questions because I feared the answers, so I just kept quiet, wondered … and worried.

Those first days were very frightening. I was facing things I'd never faced and hearing things I'd never heard. It felt as if I was traveling in a foreign land. I think I expected Anna to struggle through every procedure and especially feared the outcome of her closed-heart surgery, but everything went well and I began to think it wasn't going to be the trial I expected. Confidently I thought, *I can handle this!*

Ten days later, we were sent home and the confidence I'd gained quickly left me. Not only was I now a mother to four children (still with only two hands), but I was also dressing Anna's wounds, giving her medicine and trying to be patient when she was fussy. Because of her rapid heart rate and fast metabolism, she also required more frequent feedings. Life was beginning to overwhelm me. I just wanted to be Mommy to my four children. I wanted to read stories, fill up the pool, bake cookies and make tents in the living room. I didn't want the extra responsibilities I'd been given, but I did desperately want the little girl that required them. Every time I considered the alternative, I gained a little more courage and fought a little harder. My new baby girl was worth every effort I was required to make.

*****

It was a stressful time to move, but we wanted wide-open spaces for Anna. When she was only three months old, we moved to a charming 100-year-old home on five acres. We hoped the fresh farm air would be good for her heart, and that became my motivation as I added packing boxes to my list of responsibilities. It was a dream come true for Kyle and me. Like many men, Kyle was thrilled at the idea of "owning land!" (Charles Ingalls comes to mind.) I, on the other hand, wanted all that came with land. I wanted to watch my children chase chickens and pick wildflowers from the field. My mind held visions of large gardens and clotheslines graced with white sheets blowing in the breeze. I craved a perfectly simple life away from the city. My Lord, my five acres, my old home, my husband and my four children were my greatest sources of pleasure and joy. I was inspired to live and share a life graced with beauty and purpose.

*****

Living on an old farm with a huge red barn and an old dilapidated chicken coop was like a little piece of Heaven to me. I became an avid reader of "how-to" books and had enjoyed devouring homesteading magazines for years. I felt as if I had been in training and was now ready to try my hand at raising chickens, milking goats and growing vegetables.

Our first goat was a Nubian doe named Nellie. We bought her with her kid, Buttercup. Kyle had done a great job building a milking stand from plans we'd bought from the Internet, making milking an easy chore once we got the hang of it. (It made our hands very sore for a while.) Milking had the same satisfaction as making my own bread; however, I soon handed the chore over to Kyle, because I was so busy in the house with the children. He was happy to assume the responsibility because it provided him with a sense of accomplishment. Each day he'd come in and tell me how fast he'd milked

Nellie as he handed over the bucket of milk.

Using up the milk was not difficult. We drank it with every meal and also made ice cream, yogurt and cottage cheese. The milk was wonderful when it didn't taste like the barn, and it only did when we were lazy about keeping clean hay down for bedding.

With spring just around the corner, we decided to start the garden I'd dreamed of. I was prone to having a black thumb and was determined to overcome it. I bought a book about square-foot gardening because it seemed to be the easier way, and I was all about easy. Kyle built me my own secret garden behind our house, cutting up pallets to create a border and planting privet hedge inside that. My first year was very productive and I was *extremely* impressed with myself. I felt I had done something wonderful by tending the garden and I was happily rewarded with huge cucumbers, succulent tomatoes (of unusual varieties) and even an abundance of strawberries. I'll admit, I never expected gardening to provide such emotional satisfaction.

Pallets were some of Kyle's best friends on the farm. He had an abundant supply through work, and used them for everything from fences and compost bins to boxes for putting our baby chicks in. Our first chicks came by mail order. We ordered the minimum of 25. Kyle put the pallet chicken box in the basement and we (especially the children) anxiously awaited that delivery. The day the boxes came, we realized the mistake. Instead of sending us 25 chicks, the hatchery sent us 75! I had read that raising baby chicks often produced casualties. I don't know if we were gifted chick farmers or lucky ones, but all 75 of them survived! The unfortunate part was that we ended up with the most horrendous chicken aroma in our house. We had no way of knowing putting chickens in the basement was such a bad idea until the stench permeated our house and our noses.

Our plan had originally been to keep most of the chickens for their eggs, but also butcher a few for the experience. Since we ended up with so many, we had to butcher more than a few or we'd have eggs bursting from the fridge. We planned a chicken butchering party and invited some experienced farmers (and ex-famers) to come and help out. I videotaped the event — for educational purposes, of course — but it ended up being more along the lines of *The Great Chicken Massacre*. I ran with the video camera, screaming, as the chickens spontaneously flopped all over the place (including in my direction). Abigail enjoyed picking up the chicken heads by their cockscombs and chasing the other children with them!

Most of our chickens were friendly, but there was a Buff Orpington rooster that attacked me in the corral. Unfortunately, it happened while a truck was passing by. I'm what you might call the opposite of a mild reactor — so much so that the truck stopped and a man got out to see if I was okay. I was humiliated, to say the least! There was another rooster that scared all of us. He was the meanest rooster that ever lived — at least out here. We were so afraid of him that we wouldn't go outside for fear of being attacked. We were prisoners in our own home … all because of a rooster named Zorro! When Kyle rode his dirt bike, Zorro chased him in an effort to claim his territory. We knew that rooster had to go, and the normal way to kill a chicken is to chop off its head or break its neck. Kyle was too afraid to get a hold of his head, so he did what any master of a rebellious rooster would do. He took out his shotgun and took care of him! It was a shame we couldn't eat him. There would have been great satisfaction in that.

The country was where we were meant to be. I adored watching my little ones as they wandered around exploring their new territory. There was so much for them to discover and learn. I discovered the joy of taking walks down dirt roads, spreading my arms out to the world while dancing in the grass, and enjoying my absolute favorite activity … napping outside. The country proved to be good for more than Anna's heart … it was good for her momma's heart, too.

One thing I realized early on is that when you live in the country, people tend to take advantage of your property. We've had people drop off their scrap lumber, ask to use our property to burn their trash and cut wood from our tree row. Most of the time, Kyle was happy to oblige. I usually wasn't so happy, especially if it cluttered our farm and gave us the appearance of being rednecks.

One time we sold a buck to a Muslim family. They didn't live in the country so they asked Kyle if they could butcher the goat on our property after purchasing it. I didn't like the idea, but Kyle thought it sounded like another opportunity to learn something, so he invited the family out to our farm to butcher the goat.

Kyle and Jared watched while the men slit the goat's throat, bled it out and cut it up. I worried Jared would have nightmares, and he does admit to being a little "freaked out" over the whole ordeal, but I guess I hadn't realized yet that the male gender usually gets some strange thrill out of grotesque things (like goat killings). While the Muslim men did their manly duty, their wives and children (and I swear there were 50 of them) enjoyed our basketball goal, our kids' toys and our bathroom. The little kids even called Jared "Uncle."

"Uncle, Uncle, can we ride your bike?"

"Uncle, Uncle, where is your basketball?"

I guess killing a goat is a family affair. We even became their family! After the goat was butchered, the huge family piled all 50 (or so) people, and the pieces of the goat they didn't leave in our tree row, into their mini-van and drove away. We wouldn't forget that experience — ever!

Life on the farm was a lot of work, a ton of fun and definitely educational.

CHAPTER 2

It was an afternoon in early July 1998, and while there were probably a lot of important activities going on around me, none of them beckoned me to be a part of them. Instead, I did what any other tired husband and father would do — I took a nap. This had become a daily routine and provided a moment of peace in the middle of my hectic, but comfortable, life.

I was alone at home — my wife, Jocinda, was at work and our seven-month-old son, Taylor, was with my mom for the day. My mom was Taylor's babysitter as my wife and I tried to establish our place in the world.

I woke up, suddenly, to the sound of the phone ringing. I was alarmed and somewhat disoriented. I laid there for a second trying to decide whether I should ignore it and go back to sleep or force my body off of the couch to pick up the phone. I'm not sure why I chose to answer it, but I'm glad I did.

*****

I'd met Jo at Subway. She worked the day shift and I, the night shift. After having short conversations here and there, I knew I wanted to spend more time with her. I eventually mustered up the courage to ask her out. We began our first date at a nice Italian restaurant and eventually made our way to the bowling alley. Although it might not seem the most romantic escapade, I was a good bowler, and isn't every *pursuing-a-woman* man's goal to impress?

I think destiny shows itself rather quickly regarding love, and it certainly did with us. After dating for six months, we knew we were destined to be together and I asked Jo to marry me. Six months after our engagement, we were married. It was November '96. We didn't have a large wedding — only close friends and family — and we didn't get married on a weekend like most people would. We did something unusual. We tied the knot on a Tuesday! In one day, I went from finishing up my Psychology test to watching my bride walk down the aisle — well, in theory, anyway. She actually just stood with me in front of the judge who married us. We couldn't afford a formal wedding, so we got married in an old house in Newton, KS. We did have a couple of days off of work, so we were able to stay one night in a hotel in Wichita and go to breakfast the next morning. It wasn't much, but it was fun to be with the one I had chosen to spend my life with. As long as we were together, we were happy, and nothing else mattered.

Little did we know that three months into our marriage,

we'd be expecting our first child. We were very happy to be adding to our family and looked forward to meeting our firstborn. We didn't find out the sex of the baby, because the surprise factor appealed to us.

Our son, Taylor Gabriel, was born on November 13 of 1997, just two weeks shy of our first anniversary. He was a big baby, but still so tiny. Like most first-time parents, we were so proud of him! I've always been a very sensitive and somewhat emotional person, but this new role brought out so many fresh, unrecognized emotions.

Jo was a wonderful mother to Taylor. I loved watching her care for him and meet his needs. While taking him on long stroller rides, she'd get stopped many times by neighbors who loved to rave about his "adorable"-ness, and Jo, with her proud Mommy smile, would repeat the phrase, "Oh thank you," over and over again. We had friends at the college, which was just down the street from our house. Every week, Jo took Taylor to the girl's dormitory to watch *Melrose Place*. Taylor became somewhat of a mascot to them. He was quite the ladies man, even at a mere three months old!

While Taylor brought us a huge amount of pleasure and was our pride and joy, he also brought many sleepless nights. He had colic for many months after he was born, and while I had heard about colic, I didn't know how truly terrible it could be. I had a new respect and perhaps sympathy for parents of colicky children.

Many nights we just sat on the kitchen floor and listened

to him cry. Holding him brought no comfort, so sometimes we just left him alone. We were both working parents, so we shared the night duty. We were in it together. Besides, in our small house, it would have been impossible to sleep with all the screaming. Sometimes we were the ones crying, out of sheer desperation. A person can only go so long without sleep without reaching a certain level of insanity.

We rented the main floor of a house and our landlords lived in the basement. We were always concerned that they would ask us to move out. Being the nice people they were, they always denied hearing Taylor, but we knew better. They were a young couple and didn't have children. We were just sure they'd decide not to have any after hearing the nighttime cries of terror through their ceiling.

Eventually, we discovered a device created for babies called the Johnny Jump Up. It hung suspended from the doorframe. I couldn't believe Taylor had the ability to bounce to the heights he did. He would jump so wildly that he'd bang against the doorframe. His grandma figured out that he actually had the ability to bounce to the rhythm of the music. He enjoyed that seat so much that he wore himself out bouncing and fell asleep right there in the seat. Sometimes he'd even bounce a little in his sleep and then drop back off again.

As Taylor became less fussy and more entertaining, I could imagine watching him play football, cheering him on from the sidelines, but every new thing he learned brought new thoughts about his future to mind. I wanted the world for

Taylor, but I worried I wouldn't be everything he needed.

Even though I was very happy in my marriage and loved being a daddy, I really wasn't ready for everything fatherhood held. I already struggled with moodiness and depression (had my whole life), but functioning on so little sleep because of Taylor's colic made it worse. I had a hard time getting up to go to work and was always on edge. As a result, I did a lousy job nurturing my wife and son.

I'm sure Jo was tired, too, but she didn't react in the same way. She loved being a new mother, and despite the challenges, radiated love and joy. She didn't generally let my issues get in the way of her happiness. She knew I struggled with depression and realized very early in our marriage that I was easily affected by physical and emotional stress. Sometimes my reactions to the stress may have been perceived as coldness, but I think it was actually the deep emotions of my heart that made me struggle so much. I felt things very easily and didn't know how to assimilate and express those thoughts outwardly. I've always had a tendency to attempt to bear the burdens of those around me, but, unfortunately, I've never had the strength to manage those burdens well.

*****

I wasn't expecting a call and wondered if it might be one of the students I was tutoring. Stumbling to the phone, still half asleep, I picked it up and said, "Hello." It surprised me when I realized it was the man I had recently met while applying for a job. A couple of weeks earlier I had received a letter from him "regretting to inform" me that I wasn't being offered the position. Apparently the applicant that had been chosen didn't take the job and I was next on the list. He was obviously nervous when he asked if I was still interested in the job. Surely he knew I'd realize I was his second choice, but I surprised him by not hesitating at all. I told him, "I am absolutely still interested!"

The opportunity had come to me through a man who often came to eat at the Subway where I worked. He was a police officer who usually just came through the drive-thru, but always took time to visit for a bit. One night when he came through, he told me about a job he thought I should apply for. There was an opening for a dispatcher position at the 911 Center and he thought it would be something I'd like to do. I had never considered doing that type of work, but having watched the show *Rescue 911* on television years before, there was an element of curiosity and excitement in the idea, so I jumped at the opportunity.

After interviewing, I had received a letter of regret. I was very disappointed after getting my hopes up for the position, yet wasn't really surprised. The interview had been a little strange in that there was a whole panel of people who were asking me questions. I had also been upfront in telling them that I would only be available for about a year because I had studied pre-med and was planning to go to graduate school.

I was quite surprised and very excited when I received

the call offering me the job. I had many plans for my future, but none of them were certain, and now with a baby in tow, I wasn't sure any of those plans would work out. This new opportunity provided the extra security I needed to establish my role as a husband and father. It was a thrilling time in my life.

Jo had gone to college for several years, pursuing a career in nursing. She took a nurse's aid certification class and began working in a nursing home. She loved her new job and was very fulfilled in it. Now, with my new job, I was going to have the chance to do something I was actually interested in too. We were both very excited about the direction our life was taking.

That phone call from the man that would become my mentor and my friend was a turning point for us. On July 12, 1998, I entered the 911 Center for my first night of training. I had absolutely no idea where this new stage of our journey was going to lead.

CHAPTER 3

I've always appreciated the easiness of home — a place where I could be myself, and everybody seemed to accept who that was. When I was a child, I preferred it to every other place, except maybe Chi Chi's (one of the only places we could talk my frugal dad into taking us to eat). Some of my most treasured memories took place in our family's brick, ranch-style home in Derby, KS. Monday nights you'd find my mom, my two sisters and me lounging in our living room watching *Little House on the Prairie.* (In those days, we didn't have the option of recording the show and watching it later.) At random times, in silly moments, you'd find us girls lying on the kitchen floor having laughing contests. It was something we worked very hard at. We'd start by quickly exporting air from our lungs, which always caused our legs to rise, and eventually that air would turn into the dorkiest laugh you've ever heard. We put my overused handheld cassette player to work recording our laughs for later enjoyment. What other place than home could you get away with that type of behavior?

Even after becoming a mom, I still preferred the repose of home and abhorred having too many duties drag me away from my beloved abode. Because of Anna's fragile health, we rarely ventured out for fear of bringing illness home to her. While it might have seemed like torture to some … to be stuck at home day after day, I loved it and appreciated the excuse to be the homebody I was. I knew it couldn't last forever, but while Anna was little, I'd do everything in my power to keep her healthy.

Anna was the center of all of our attention. She was held, laughed at, tickled and doted over on a daily basis. Making her smile was a priority and we were constantly in competition to see who could produce a hearty laugh. I'd put her in her colorful saucer-seat and the kids would bring her practically every toy we owned. It was so cute that we'd take pictures of her about to be lost in the mountain of colorful toys.

Our house faces south and has 27 windows. It doesn't matter what room you're in, you can see the beautiful outdoors without any effort at all. One thing I love about my windows is that they are all very tall, reaching almost from floor to ceiling. The kids can look out without having to crawl up on anything. I've watched the sunrise over and over again through the wall of windows in my dining room. On numerous occasions I've run outside, even in bare feet on a cold morning, just to snap a picture of the sky. Our barn is often silhouetted in front of the sunrises.

Our property has the most delightful tree row. It's been the setting for many childhood adventures. Jared and Abigail pretended it was Sherwood Forest and Narnia and videotaped themselves acting out their own stories from their imagined worlds. We've buried beloved pets in the tree row, dug up many treasures (because 100 years ago people used to bury their trash), and sung by the campfire while roasting marshmallows until they were black!

When we moved to our old farm, Kyle became consumed in projects. He spent hour upon hour working to make our old homestead nice, or in some cases just livable. He often had Jared by his side, handing him tools or running to get him a glass of tea. I drank it all in. I loved watching each member of my family enjoy their little piece of our farm.

There was a point when the newness of my captivating life wore off just enough to not be so distracting. When this happened, I once again began to worry about what was ahead for Anna and for us. I avoided the thoughts as long as I could, but Anna's first open-heart surgery was approaching and I feared it. She was only nine months old. How could a person so little survive something so big? I couldn't wrap my mind around it and my heart couldn't contain the emotion. I'd begin to wonder if we'd lose her, and then I'd push the thoughts from my mind.

I knew where to go for help, and I fell to my knees on many occasions. I always felt better when I managed to pray, but there were many times when I just sat and wondered

… and worried. I asked myself, *What's the worst thing that can happen,* in hopes of relieving my anxiety, but when it involves your baby girl, that method of therapy doesn't provide any consolation. My heart struggled with thoughts of losing Anna. I loved her so dearly, and the possibility of living without her wasn't something I could think about without becoming very anxious. Each time I sought the Lord, He gave me the strength to endure … and to hope. I wished I could always be faithful to seek Him and never fret, but it just wasn't possible. I think I had to fret before I thought to run to the Lord.

*****

The day we took Anna to Kansas City for her open-heart surgery, I not only had her on my mind, but also my almost nine-year-old son, Jared. He was such a tender, emotional and often fearful child, and the night before we left, he begged us to take him with us. I knew he was scared that Anna would die, but I also knew he was worried about me. I think that firstborn children want to take care of things — a responsibility that should never belong to a child. He felt very insecure when he didn't have at least a little bit of control over a situation. I considered taking him with us, but I knew I'd be torn between my two children and Anna would need me by her side. I also didn't want to subject Jared to the world I was imagining. It was a frightening and sad place.

My mother's heart was tormented. I was being dragged away from three of my children and forced to take my fourth to what I had pictured as a living hell.

I had to continually take my cares to the Lord and just trust that He would take care of Jared and the girls while I was gone. They'd have their grandma and grandpa and plenty to keep them busy while we were away. There were goats to milk, chickens to feed, meals to help Grandma with, cats to play with, schoolwork to do, and a multitude of other chores and activities.

The anticipation of the surgery about drove me out of my mind. We stayed in a hotel in Kansas City the night before Anna was to be admitted. If I slept at all, it wasn't much. I kept thinking that night might be the last one I had with Anna. I pushed those thoughts out of my mind every time, but they kept creeping back in. I was told that Anna couldn't have breast milk after midnight and I worried about how she'd handle that. As was her routine, she woke up in the night to nurse. By some miracle, I was able to give her about three ounces of apple juice in a bottle. She'd never had apple juice and had never taken a bottle before, so I couldn't believe she did that night. I acknowledged it as God showing me that He was taking care of even the minutest details, and it did increase my faith, at least for a while.

In the early morning, we headed to the hospital. There was a lot of prep work to be done and I remember one particular female doctor who made me angry. She was so rough with Anna and very rude to us. Dealing with people like that made it so much harder to cope. The only consolation to being at the hospital was that we were getting closer to the end of what I had pictured as the most horrific event of my life.

Because Anna was so young, they decided not to sedate her before taking her from us. I had no opinion about what was best, but when the operating room nurse came for her, I suddenly had an opinion and wished she had been sedated. It unfolded very much like I'd imagined it would. We stood clinging to each other at the end of a long white hallway ... tears pouring from my eyes and sobs involuntarily escaping my body. Our daughter seemed smaller than she ever had as she was being carried away to an unknown world that was on the other side of two large white doors. White walls, white floor, white everything. Anna was afraid and screamed for us all the way down the hall. My heart felt as though it was being violently ripped from my chest. When they passed through the double doors and we could no longer see her, I could still hear her cry. I wanted to run to her and take her away from them. Kyle put his arm firmly around me and guided me into the waiting room where we sat snuggled up close to each other and let the tears fall.

We suffered in that waiting room for many hours. Knowing what was taking place in the operating room was what made the waiting so hard. We knew they were cutting open Anna's chest, putting her on a heart/lung bypass machine and attempting to work on her tiny heart. While we were waiting,

I frantically wrote in my journal. I vented, feared and hoped on those pages, penning my prayers to the Lord. I knew I wouldn't survive my thoughts and emotions if I didn't add God to the mix. My past experiences with tragedy and heartache reminded me that the most important thing to do was to cry out to God. I knew that He would bring peace as I did so.

We periodically received updates throughout the surgery, and called home to inform our family each time we were given news. Finally, after many hours of waiting, the nurse told us that Anna's surgery had gone well. They were getting ready to remove the ventilator. In Anna's first surgery they had accessed her heart by cutting a slit between her ribs, but this surgery required her chest to be opened. We knew the recovery would be longer, but were willing to endure anything as long as we were able to take Anna home with us. When the nurse, Beth, brought the good news, we praised God! Tears of relief poured out. We called home and told my parents and the kids that everything had gone well, and rejoiced as we heard the relief in their voices. After so many hours, they were so glad to finally hear! They'd been sitting at home, anxiously awaiting our calls.

Beth came back just moments later. The expression on her face was much different than it had been before. I thought I saw pity on her face and it scared me. Our questioning eyes brought the words, "Anna got very sick." Beth then explained to us that when they removed the ventilator, Anna stopped breathing and her heart quit beating. They had to work hard to get her heart started again, but they eventually did and then reinserted the ventilator. We were told, "Anna is very critical. Prepare yourselves, she might not live."

*****

During those days in the hospital, we desperately clung to the Lord. I continued to journal many times a day. It was a perfect way to express my thoughts without burdening Kyle. Kyle was the only one with me, and he was dealing with his own fear and anxiety. His way of coping was escaping. He spent his time reading C.S. Lewis and J.R.R. Tolkien books. I was glad we both had a way to deal with the stress.

There was a part of me that just wanted God to take Anna. I didn't want this to drag out for weeks or months to an end filled with heartache. At least if Anna died, she wouldn't be suffering and we could move on. Yet I also begged God to spare her life — no matter what it took.

Anna spent day after day so still and lifeless. We suffered as we watched her oxygen saturation drop and her blood pressure rise too high and then drop too low. She had fluid on her lungs, irregular heart rhythms, low blood counts and began to get bedsores on the back of her swollen head. When she wasn't getting any better, the doctors knew they had to do something, so even though she wasn't stable, they took Anna for another heart catheterization. The results showed them that the first surgery had created an obstruction in her pulmonary veins. They'd have to go back in to attempt to correct it. The next surgery would hopefully correct the obstruction and allow her blood to flow freely. If it didn't work, she would die.

We hoped that day and we feared that day. Only time would tell. After waiting anxiously in the Ronald McDonald family room for what seemed like an eternity, we were finally put out of our misery. The surgeon walked in and told us that everything had gone according to plan and that he thought Anna would recover. Since I couldn't fly, I just let my spirit soar.

We grew to love and respect many of Anna's nurses and doctors. They fought so hard to make her well and yet treated her so tenderly. We hated to say goodbye to them, but we were very happy when we were told we could go home. We spent a total of three weeks at the hospital and had experienced things we'd hoped we could have been ignorant of for the rest of our lives. Anna did survive that horrible ordeal and returned to our home filled with siblings who loved and missed her. She returned to farm life that begged her to be a part of it: flowers to be picked by her little fingers, dirt to be trampled by her tiny feet and animals to be squeezed by her loving arms. Life once again became incredibly precious to my family and me. We had endured the greatest trial of our lives and were able to claim a victory!

CHAPTER 4

I arrived at the Dispatch Center a little early my first day. I wanted to have some extra time to get settled and was anxious to make a good impression. My routine had never involved a night shift, so I was concerned about whether I would be able to stay alert all night.

Three to four months of training was ahead of me, and I was a little worried about the implications of that. I hadn't anticipated that answering phones and talking on the radio would be complicated enough to warrant that much training! When I met my trainer, I immediately realized how seriously she took her work. I sensed that it wasn't going to be pleasant by the way she communicated. Her determined demeanor made me feel very insecure. She gave me the impression that I was in the way and she'd rather be doing something else. As I sat at the console and looked around, I noticed a room filled with computers, printers and panels of lights. There were maps on the walls and binders I could only assume held information I'd eventually have to know. I realized then that there was more to 911 dispatching than I had ever expected.

There were a couple of other people in the room and they were completely engrossed in their work. They seemed to be carrying on multiple conversations at one time. I could see that this job was going to be a challenge and I wondered if I'd made the right decision.

After my trainer got herself organized, she began the process of showing me what things were and how they worked. Having spent several years in college, I concentrated very hard and diligently took notes. I knew how to learn and felt I was in my element when I was taking in information and breaking it down so I could understand and apply it. Because I enjoyed learning, I began to settle into my training with a little less anxiety.

I was in the middle of writing something down when my trainer stopped, looked at me and asked, "Is that a beer?" I looked at her, surprised and perplexed. I had no idea what she was talking about. I saw her look past me so I followed her gaze. She had spotted the energy drink I picked up on the way to work (the one I hoped would keep me awake through the night). Looking at it, I realized that it actually did look like a beer with its tall silver can. I nervously laughed and said, "Ah, that's just my energy drink." I picked it up, turned the can around and showed it to her. I expected her to laugh, but she didn't. She just turned back to her notebook and continued presenting the information to me. I turned away from her to place the can back on the table and silently mouthed the word "Okaaay." I awkwardly turned back around and continued to take notes. It was going to be a long night.

Despite the rocky start, I decided I really liked the work. Eventually, I became comfortable with my trainer. Under her tough exterior, I found her to be a delightful and humorous woman. She was good at dispatching and proved to be a very thorough teacher. The first month of night shift was packed with learning! The center dispatched all emergency services in the county, so I learned about police, fire and EMS operations. I learned how to operate and properly talk on the 911 telephone and multi-channel radio systems. I learned about the computer databases, the emergency medical dispatch protocol, the severe weather sirens, the alarm systems, local maps, and the mountain of policies and procedures that went along with all of it. It was a complicated operation and I realized that countless mistakes could be made if I didn't learn it well.

After the first month of training, I was sent to the day shift to work with a different trainer and a different group of dispatchers. It was a time to build experience with higher call volumes and different tasks. After some time there, I moved to the evening shift to experience even higher call volumes and more critical law enforcement calls. I loved the urgent nature and fast pace of the evening shift, but when I graduated from training, I was sent back to the night shift. I knew I'd miss the busy evenings, but was content working a job I enjoyed.

While working on my own, I began to understand that it

wasn't all excitement and adrenaline rushes. I don't think any training could have prepared me for the emotional side of the work. It was shocking to realize how much violence existed in our small community. I hated to face the hard truth that men really did beat their wives and children. I didn't know how pervasive alcohol and drug abuse was and what the horrible consequences of that abuse were. I couldn't believe mental illness was so common, and was sad to come to terms with how many of those cases tragically ended in suicide.

There is no training to prepare a person for a time when he's called to comfort a woman who is reporting that her husband has just shot himself. It was almost impossible to know what to say after hearing the words, "I think he's dead." It's heart-wrenching to hear the pain expressed in the moans of devastated men and women whose lives have been forever changed by the tragedies they've experienced.

*****

One of my early experiences with tragedy occurred on a cold winter morning. I was working the night shift and my partner was on his lunch break. It was that time of night when the bridges begin to ice over slightly, but the roads appear to be clear. This is the most dangerous time because the hazards aren't yet apparent. I received a call about an accident on the highway and the caller said there was a woman lying on the road. He believed she was dead and he was right. The victim had died before the call was placed. When the officers checked her driver's license, I learned it was a woman I knew who was married to a high school friend of mine, and they had a small child.

I went to her funeral and saw firsthand how her death had affected my friend. He was devastated. That was when I began putting faces with the people I was talking to. These callers and the victims had personal lives, families and dreams that were being crushed. That first tragedy made me come to terms with the fact that these people were in a tremendous amount of pain. It was a point when I began to experience a new dimension in 911 dispatching.

*****

I found my new job to be extremely fulfilling. Jocinda had also obtained a new position — at the local hospital as a CNA. After working a while with surgical patients, she was given the opportunity to spend some of her time working in the maternal child unit, which was a dream come true for her. Her mom had worked as a nurse in the same type of unit and Jo had always aspired to work with mothers and babies. As a natural caregiver at home as well as at work, I knew she would be perfect for the job, and I was happy to see her doing something she loved.

As rewarding and enjoyable as it was for Jo, it was also very difficult when a baby died or was born sick. Tragedy is always difficult and sad, regardless of the age of the victim, but when it's an innocent, vulnerable little one, it seems so much more unfortunate. Jo's heartstrings were tugged many times as she cared for those sick babies. Sometimes she was on duty when a baby was stillborn, and she and her co-workers had the sad duty of bathing and dressing the baby. They quietly observed family members and friends taking pictures of the baby in their parent's arms, where they fit so perfectly. They gently pressed their hands and feet onto special ink-pads to make prints for the birth certificate and for the baby books. The CNAs showed those babies love, and attempted to care for the parents' broken hearts during their first hours of experiencing such extreme loss.

I had dealt with calls involving child abuse, but Jo saw this abuse in a different form. There were times when a baby was born sick and needed extended care. Most parents couldn't stand to be away, but many times Jo witnessed babies who were left alone without parental care and love. Some parents were too wrapped up in their own lives and addictions to love and care for the child they'd just brought into the world. There were so many innocent victims of adult immaturity.

Jo and I didn't talk much about the things we dealt with in our work. Sometimes I could tell that something had happened, but she didn't usually want to talk at those times. I think she spent more time than I know, crying on her pillow, grieving in silence and solitude over those babies. I don't know if she preferred suffering on her own or if she just felt I was too wrapped up in my own life to be useful to her. I never neglected Jo on purpose, but I know I did neglect her.

By appearances, our little family was doing well. Not only did Jo and I both have jobs we enjoyed, but we had just bought our first house — a small one that really did have the proverbial white picket fence everybody seems to mention when they dream of that first home. We also had a beautiful son who brought us a lot of joy and laughter. I'd take Taylor outside with me to do yard work and he'd pretend he was helping me. I'd mow the lawn and he'd follow me with his toy mower. He'd seen me get mad at the mower for getting hung up in the grass one too many times, so he'd copy me by throwing his mower and scolding it for not working properly. When I'd see him do that I'd realize how closely he was watching me, and it scared me. I worried about Taylor learning all of my bad habits. Life was pleasant on the surface and likely appeared perfect to all who were watching, but what people couldn't see was what was going on in my heart and mind.

As I'd done off and on my whole life, I continued to fluctuate between emotional highs and lows. I was withdrawn and caught up in my own interests. I spent a lot of time watching movies, sometimes two or three in a row. Horror flicks had a way of completely sucking me in and pulling me away from my thoughts. I would find myself entranced and enjoyed the automatic physical response to the creepy scenes. It caused a sort of adrenaline rush I seemed to enjoy. The dramas I watched had the opposite effect. They seemed to appeal to my emotional side and consoled my troubled spirit. Those shows were a sort of friend to me — a friend who seemed to understand that life wasn't easy.

I listened to all genres of music, depending on my mood. Music is so stimulating to the emotions and I seemed to turn to it for consolation, comfort and whatever else I needed at the time. I often chose to listen to heavy metal music. I convinced myself that it was a cathartic activity — one that would allow me to deal with my emotions by a somewhat aggressive means. I'd convinced myself it was therapeutic, but I never felt better when I moved on to the next activity. I played computer games, read and did crossword puzzles, too. I didn't like still, quiet moments. I always had to occupy my mind with something. Despite my busy schedule, I felt I had to fit these activities in. Sometimes it was at the expense of adequate sleep and often at the expense of spending time with my family.

I didn't actually enjoy any of those activities all that much. I pursued them for the sake of distraction. I was looking for ways to get out of my head. If I let myself begin to think, I usually found fear, anxiety and dread. I sought overstimulation as a therapy. It wasn't a get-well therapy. It was more like a painkiller — one that would temporarily ease the symptoms but only cover up the real issues. I hated this about myself. It wasn't the way I wanted to be. I wanted to provide the world for my Jo and Taylor. I wanted to make them happy. I desperately wanted to be different and wanted to change. I just didn't know how to do it.

CHAPTER 5

After we had gone through so much with Anna, I half expected to get some relief, but with regular life resuming, so did the irritations and little mishaps of it. Unfortunately, poor little Anna seemed to be the victim of many of those mishaps.

Having the Internet while living in the country used to be a challenge. The only way we had access was through the phone line. Our 2,800-square-foot, two-story house only had three phone jacks — one in the kitchen, one upstairs in a bedroom and one in the dining room. Since our computer was not near any of the phone jacks, we made it work by plugging in a very long extension cord and running it across the room to plug it into our computer. We knew it was careless to leave the cord across the floor like that, but we never imagined it would cause an accident.

Kyle was walking through the room holding Anna, tripped over that cord and landed on Anna's leg. In denial, he kept telling me she was fine, but I knew she wasn't. She couldn't even stand on her leg. We took her to the doctor the next morning and discovered she had a broken femur. Our doctor sent us over to a specialist, who asked us accusing questions about how it happened. I know it's their job to do that, but it sure doesn't feel good to a parent who is already feeling guilty about it. The whole thing crushed Kyle, but Anna did get a pretty, bright pink, full-leg cast.

Another time, Anna came to me and said she felt "gaggy." When I realized she was getting ready to throw up, I grabbed a bowl. I was horrified when I saw bright red blood in the bowl. I panicked and immediately called the doctor to ask him what to do. He said that I needed to take her to the emergency room. Kyle was on his way to Kansas City on business, so I called him and asked him to meet us at the hospital, and then called my parents. My dad went with me while my mom stayed with the other children.

When we got to the hospital, we were treated poorly, as if they thought we'd done something to Anna. When the doctor listened to her heart with his stethoscope, he was quite impressed with himself as he said, "Did you know she has a very loud heart murmur?" I was thinking, *DUH!* "Of course we do, look at her chest!" They didn't treat us with any respect until our doctor talked to them and told them that we were good parents.

After a CT Scan, Anna was diagnosed with a blockage in her intestine. They told us that she would need surgery, but that vomiting bright red blood had nothing to do with the blockage — that it was a coincidence. I began to be suspicious. Anna hadn't had pain of any kind. Her only symptom was vomiting fresh blood. When they tried to explain the situation to us, it didn't make any sense. The symptoms that were associated with a blocked intestine were severe, and Anna didn't have any of them.

In case she needed surgery, they wouldn't allow Anna to drink anything — not even water — but they were extremely slow about administering her I.V. to provide fluids for her body. She was so thirsty that she begged for water. Since orders were to not let her have anything, the nurse suggested I use a washcloth to wet her lips. When I put the cloth up to her mouth, Anna began to suck the water out of it. I was delighted for her, as her thirst was relieved. When nobody was around, I soaked the washcloth with water again, but made sure it was dripping heavily. Every time the nurse walked back in, I'd pretend I was simply wiping Anna's face with it.

That whole incident ended up being a fluke — only a posterior nosebleed, of all things! I couldn't understand why this poor child of mine had to experience these unrelated issues, but they were small in comparison to what she'd already endured.

*****

Because of what we'd gone through, I really did have a zeal for life, but I had also come to realize how little I was in control of it. I knew I was to live fully, love passionately and follow God fervently, but I also knew it was imperative that I acknowledged who was in control of life, death and providence. My part was very important to God, but very small in the large scope of things.

I had watched my two baby boys die. I had watched my baby girl barely hang on to life for three weeks. I knew life was a gift and that I was *not* in control of it. If God chose to take a life or spare one, it was up to Him, not me. So I enjoyed each day, but also acknowledged that I was only in control of how I spent my days, not how many days I or my loved ones had to spend.

Being a home-schooling family and having all the children with me every day allowed us to have time for a variety of activities. We opened our textbooks out of necessity, but opened the entertaining books for inspiration and fun. The kids enjoyed pretending they were with the Ingalls family in their covered wagon, with the milkman on his milk route, helping Miss Rumphius plant her lupines and walking to town with the Ox-Cart man. They rolled their eyes with frustration over the Poky Little Puppy's distracted little brain, and scolded Peter Rabbit for not obeying his momma. What good is it to listen to a story if you can't enter into the world you're reading about? All my kids loved books and I read the same ones over and over again. In fact, they'd heard them so many times that I'd leave out the endings of the sentences and let them finish them for me.

We did the chores, but made plenty of time for fun. We created charming little tea parties using my old mismatched teacups and saucers, and grabbed a couple of teapots from my small collection. I always made our favorite chocolate chip tea scones and sometimes little sandwiches or other little tea party dainties. Tea was always in one teapot, but I often brought in another teapot full of hot water so we could drink General Foods International Coffee. Sometimes we'd get dressed up and make it a formal event, but most of the time we'd have the tea party in our regular clothes or even our pajamas. We lived a very serendipitous life — letting one spontaneous event lead to another great discovery of some sort.

Every spring we had a yard full of beautiful yellow dandelions that the kids loved to pick and bring in to me. So many people poison their little yellow flowers, but I've always thought a yard covered with dandelions was very pretty. They're such a bright yellow and grow so profusely, how could I help but love them? I had heard they were edible, but had never been brave enough to eat one. I decided to do a little research and see if that information was true. After all, I *had* attained country-girl status and was supposed to know about the little secrets of nature, right? I pulled out one of my big "how-to" books — *The Encyclopedia of Country Living* — and searched the index for "dandelions." I knew there'd be something, but was surprised to see just how much there was! Amongst many other things, I discovered dandelions could be fried — which sounded delicious — and even made into jelly, which just sounded interesting. So, I set out to try both.

The kids had such a wonderful time picking those pretty little flowers! Anna was almost two years old and was determined to do everything her brother and sisters did, so I sent them all out with their little baskets and just watched from the porch. They were bent over with their bottoms in the air for quite some time. The sun shone on their hair and they really did look like a perfect little scene out of an old-fashioned book. My cute, chubby son with his country-boy crew cut and my three precious daughters with their braids and piggy tails were tugging at dandelions with their fat little fingers and dropping them into their baskets.

When they brought their baskets in, brimming to the rim with the pretty yellow weeds, we went to the dining room table and cut the petals from the stems. It was a tedious step in the process, but one that couldn't be skipped for making the jelly. We put the flower petals in the boiling water to let them steep.

In the meantime, we decided to fry some of the dandelions up for lunch. We pinched the stems away from the flowers, then washed the flowers in a colander. We made an egg batter for dipping them in and then we fried them in oil. After removing them to a plate with a paper towel and salting them, we began to enjoy a tasty delicacy, at least that's how we felt about it — fried dandelions really are delightful!

The jelly was quite good, too, and I made it two years in a row (and gave it to friends in Christmas baskets), but it does require quite a bit more work so we've decided to stick with the fried dandelions. We look forward to them every spring!

*****

I'm not sure how it came about initially. Perhaps one of our kids questioned the same thing I did as a child. You see, I never understood why there was a Father's Day and a Mother's Day but not a Kids' Day. When I was a child, I'd asked my parents about it many times. Their answer was always, "Every day is Kids' Day!" The only problem I had with that was that if every day was Kids' Day, why wasn't every day Mother's Day and Father's Day? It didn't make the least bit of sense to me. I always knew there should be a "Kids' Day," so I proclaimed, "Let's create one!"

Our first Kids' Day was so much fun. Kyle took the day off work and we all played! (and I mean played) We had bike races, Frisbee-throwing contests, obstacle courses, water fights, fun snacks and even prizes. The kids absolutely loved our first Kids' Day. It would be the first of many.

*****

I would have been perfectly happy if life would have remained just like it was. I had children of all ages and loved

43

every stage of childhood. I was blessed with a hardworking husband who loved being a daddy and got involved with everything the kids did.

I knew Anna needed another surgery, but once again, I tried very hard not to think about it. I had Anna with me and she was doing well. There was no need to worry about her future while she was thriving. The time would come when I wouldn't be able to help it, and I'd worry then. For the time being, though, I decided I'd just be a busy, happy, content momma. Life was extremely satisfying and sweet, and I was going to do everything in my power to keep it that way.

CHAPTER 6

"Court, we need to talk." Jo had a very serious look on her face. I wasn't sure if I was in trouble or what, but she had that tone that told me it was something important. She led me to the bedroom and we sat together on the edge of the bed.

As I sat there wondering what was on Jo's mind, she stated boldly, "I think it's time to have another baby." This didn't come as a surprise to me. We'd been casually talking about it for quite some time, but I'd convinced her that I wasn't ready. We'd been enjoying Taylor so much and I was afraid I wouldn't be able to effectively father two children. I already felt so inadequate. My appeals had worked every other time, but Jo was ready to take a stand.

Jo explained all the logic behind her desire and I tried to listen with an open mind and heart. She had a point when she said, "Taylor's almost four now. I don't want him to be an only child and I don't want a big gap between our children. Court, we're missing our opportunity." I knew she was right, but those sleepless nights of never-ending screaming were the first things that came to mind. I had no desire to go back. They were long and they were hard! I remembered feeling like a rotten, impatient parent when I couldn't console my own son. It wasn't until Taylor got beyond his colic that I finally began to feel somewhat competent in my parenting.

It was obvious that Jo had planned out the whole conversation very carefully. She had an answer to every question I had. There was no way to convince her otherwise, and by the end of the conversation, I'd agreed to her plan. We'd have a baby "as soon as possible!" Before I agreed, I did state one condition. I asked that she not work the night shift because if I had any choice in the matter, I would *not* go through those sleepless nights again — ever! I felt sort of guilty making that request and followed it with my head slightly turned, my eyes squinted and a guilty grin on my face. When she happily agreed, I turned towards her and smiled big and sincere.

Jocinda's wish for "as soon as possible" was easily accomplished. After just a few months we were told that she was pregnant. I'll admit, I was still worried about those sleepless nights, feeling that somehow I was going to be roped into staying up with a colicky baby again, but truth be told, I was really excited! I wasn't sure how all of the details of childcare would work out with two little ones, but the excitement of the pregnancy took care of all of that and I decided I'd take it one step at a time. We'd be okay.

*****

Jo was very sick through the first half of her pregnancy and missed many days of work because of it. I'm sure it was discouraging and I felt bad for worrying so much about myself, especially after watching her suffer through such horrible nausea. She was scheduled for a sonogram at her halfway point — 20 weeks — and that was fast approaching. I hoped that seeing our little baby for the first time would overshadow the discomfort she had.

Since we'd experienced the surprise of not knowing the sex of our baby ahead of time with the first, we decided we wanted to find out the sex of this baby. That way we'd have both experiences under our belt! While I would have been thrilled with another boy, I was hoping for a girl. I can't put my finger on why, but the thought of having a little girl just melted my heart.

The day of the sonogram finally came and all we were thinking about was what we were going to have. We had no fears or worries at all. The first glimpses of our baby brought us so much joy and excitement. Everything appeared to be just perfect! It seemed to take forever, but eventually the technician said what we'd been waiting to hear: "Do you want to know the sex of your baby?" My answer was a hearty, "You bet!" She then proceeded to tell us it was a baby girl! I'll never forget that moment. Jo and I looked at each other, beaming with joy. Our dream was coming true. I'm sure I was glowing as the technician handed me some pictures to take home. She finished up the measurements and observations that would be sent to the doctor and then told us that everything looked "just right," except for the size of our baby's head. It was larger than it should be. It kind of threw me because she hadn't acted as if anything was wrong. Why hadn't she let on before then? I became upset with her for not being open with us. She wouldn't elaborate on the implications of that measurement, but both Jo and I sensed that it caused her some concern. Our elation diminished as we began to consider the meaning of the strange news.

That evening, I began to research on the Internet what might be going on with our baby. There were a number of conditions that could result in a large sized head and none of them sounded like anything I'd be comfortable with. However, I didn't lose all hope because I'd also read that it could be an anomaly that wouldn't persist. I told myself that these methods of diagnosis weren't foolproof. I knew we'd just have to wait to hear what the doctor said at our next appointment.

I hated that Jo had to go to the follow-up appointment alone, but I was driving a cab part-time in the mornings and couldn't get out of work. I also hated that I had to work two jobs, but it seemed that there was always debt we were trying to pay off. I just couldn't seem to get a hold of our finances.

I was anxious to get home and talk to Jo. As soon as I saw her, I could tell she was upset. I asked her what was wrong and she said, "Our baby has Bilateral Choroid Plexus cysts." Obviously, that meant absolutely nothing to me. When Jo saw my surprised look, she continued, "It's very uncommon — only about one percent of babies have it, and in about half of those babies it goes away on its own before delivery." It was the other half that neither of us could ignore. BCPC could also be an indication of Down's Syndrome or Trisomy 18. The doctor told Jo that our baby might be fine, but also warned that she may die in the womb or shortly after birth. There really was no way to predict what would happen.

At a later appointment, our doctor reviewed his concerns with us. He offered the option of an amniocentesis. With that test we'd be able to know if our baby had a chromosome disorder, but after asking the doctor if there was any therapeutic value in the procedure and hearing his reply of "No," we emphatically denied the test. We knew there were risks involved that we weren't willing to take. There might be those who would abort at this point and I knew that was technically an option, but not for us. We'd never take our child's life, even if there was a serious problem involved. No, we'd just wait. But the waiting was torture.

*****

We continued to wait … another nine weeks before we would go for the next sonogram. Those nine weeks were stressful and somewhat sad days. We wanted to hope, but how could we not consider the worst-case scenario? Jo and I didn't talk about it much. It just seemed to be our way.

Besides, what was there to say? We'd only bring each other down. I could tell it was weighing on her and I'm certain she could see the same when she looked my way. Those days were rough for both of us.

It went very slowly, but eventually the nine-week wait was over and we were at a point in the pregnancy and baby's development where we would be able to determine what was going on with our baby girl. I made sure I was able to go to that appointment; I wouldn't have missed it. I was so anxious to be on to the next phase of this ordeal! I wanted to know more. I couldn't stand being stuck in the world of the unknown.

We weren't able to use our local hospital for this sonogram. We had to travel about 30 minutes to Wichita to have the level-2 sonogram. This had to be done on more sophisticated equipment. We spent those 30 minutes in the car in near silence.

Jo's name was called. The sonographer had our paperwork and knew exactly why we were there. I sat next to Jo, both of us waiting anxiously as the test began. The sonographer viewed our baby's head in detail and took careful measurements. To our surprise, she suddenly announced, "No evidence of cysts!" They had completely resolved! The emotion that overtook us was wonderful! We banked on our doctor's statement that said, "If the cysts are gone, there shouldn't be any problems." In our minds, we were home-free! We couldn't wait to go and announce to our family and friends that our baby was okay.

*****

The rest of the pregnancy flew by for us. Being happy moves time so much more quickly than being worried. We were so excited to bring our baby home. Taylor couldn't stop asking, "When is baby coming?" We had a middle name picked, but we hadn't settled on a first name for our daughter. We were vacillating between Ashley and Hannah. Ashley Paige was the name we picked for a girl when Jo was pregnant with Taylor. Taylor couldn't say Ashley, but he could say Hannah, so Taylor made the decision for us. We decided on Hannah Paige.

Jo was in her 37th week of pregnancy and had just worked a busy evening shift. She'd helped to deliver four babies that night and came home beat. She was having contractions, but nothing very regular. She tried to sleep, but was up and down all night wondering if she was in labor. Finally, a little before 7:00 am, she woke me up and said, "It's time to go to the hospital." I woke up fast that morning.

Once we were in the observation room, the nurse checked Jo and she was only dilated to 2 centimeters. We walked the halls for 30 minutes and she made it to 3 centimeters. At about 8:00 am, the doctor broke her water and she quickly progressed to 5 centimeters. Jo planned to have medication to manage her pain, but wasn't sure when she wanted to get it. She seemed to slow down a little in her progress and the doctor thought it'd be a while, so Jo sent Taylor and I to the cafeteria to get some breakfast.

When we got back to the room, Jo's condition had changed.

She was very uncomfortable and told me to get her nurse. When the nurse checked her, she was dilated to 7 centimeters. Jo and the nurse decided it was time to get the epidural, but the anesthesiologist was busy and couldn't get to the room right then. In another 30 short minutes, Jo was fully dilated and was out of time for the epidural. Her doctor was notified and the nurses were rushing around getting everything ready for the delivery. I think we were both surprised at how quickly everything moved along and probably a little scared too — especially Jo. I became a little nervous when I realized we still had Taylor and there wasn't anybody there to watch him, but my parents showed up just in time to take him out into the hallway to wait for Hannah to be born.

The baby was crowning and the nurse said it looked like she would have to deliver her without our doctor. Luckily, he showed up just in time to deliver Hannah, who was born at 10:49 am on August 11, 2001. She was big for an early baby — 8 pounds, 6 ounces and 21 inches long. She was adorable and I was a proud daddy. This little girl would certainly have me wrapped around her little finger.

Taylor was so excited to have a baby sister; it had been a long wait for a little boy. When his grandparents tried to snatch him away to take him home with them, he threw a fit. I'm sure he felt he deserved to stay. So, that first night, I slept in the recliner next to Jo and Hannah, and Taylor slept on the couch. We were a perfect little family of four, together for the first time. I'm sure Jo was exhausted from the delivery, but for me, it was just a perfect night.

Two days later, Hannah was doing well and we all got to go home together. To my surprise, and admittedly my relief, Hannah was a perfectly content baby. She was so easy to care for. No sleepless nights! She was peaceful and happy. All of my fears were gone. My sweet baby didn't have Bilateral Choroid Plexus cysts or any other disease. Hannah's health was good and she was not colicky. I was so glad Jo was firm with me when telling me it was time for another baby. Had she let me have my way, I wouldn't have been blessed with this beautiful daughter of mine, my Hannah Paige.

CHAPTER 7

Four Years Later ...

I technically 'schooled' the children right through the summer, but the children and I felt a greater sense of freedom during those months. I've always used our *summer school* to teach things that I find infinitely more interesting, things that are discovered spontaneously — out of curiosity — and usually outdoors.

Because Anna's birthday was in the summer, her celebrations often involved fresh flowers, outdoor pictures, little plastic swimming pools and outdoor games. We were all looking forward to another celebration of Anna's life — a special gift to our family.

Anna was very mature for a six-year-old, but that's not really surprising considering all she'd endured. Trials seem to have a way of growing us up. I'd grown up too. Two little brothers had been added to our family — Silas and Jonas. Anna mothered them very sincerely by scolding them, nurturing them and even rolling her eyes at their orneriness, but Abigail was my biggest helper because she could change diapers.

While it wasn't something we planned, it seemed that we were left with three pair of children. Jared and Abigail spent most of their time together, as did Cecily and Anna, and Silas and Jonas. While they all loved playing together, it was convenient that they all kind of had their own sibling to spend their time with. Jared and Abigail spent many hours drinking hot chocolate, putting together puzzles and listening to audio dramas (all at the same time!). Cecily and Anna were often found pretending to be Laura and Mary Ingalls. One time I peeked in the room where they were playing together and I saw Anna on Silas' toddler bed pretending she was having a baby and Cecily putting a cloth to her head, telling her, "Breathe, Mary. It's okay, just breathe!" I had to walk away so I could laugh without them hearing me.

They all played games together, listened to music, danced, sang, watched movies, and even pulled out the video camera and did their own "Kraft Productions." Jared often recruited all of his brothers and sisters to play roles in his movies. Kyle and I had to stifle our laughter as we watched his amateur attempt at movie making, but we were also impressed with his creativity and we encouraged him to keep using his amazing imagination.

After Anna turned four, we took her to Kansas City for an evaluation to see if she was ready for her next surgery — the completion of the Fontan. We were told that the pressures in her lungs were too high and they feared the surgery would worsen her condition. It wasn't good news because she needed that surgery, but I did feel somewhat relieved for not having to go through it. Despite Anna's heart not looking so well to the doctors, her health had been very good through the years. Then, right before her sixth birthday, Anna's health took a strange turn. Her new symptoms caused me a great deal of stress. There were a few times when her heart would start to beat very quickly as though it was panicked. She also began to look very swollen, especially in her face and limbs. One day she said in a slightly worried tone, "Mom, my heart's beating weird." I instantly panicked emotionally and physically, but then she laughed and said, "I'm just teasing!" I knew she wasn't, but that was just how she was. As soon as I worried, she tried to ease my mind. After a trip to her cardiologist, we felt better. He didn't think it was anything to be very concerned with. After a thorough examination he said that everything looked "pretty much the same." I tried to gain confidence from that, but being Anna's momma, I knew something was different and it constantly caused me to worry.

It was also during this time that Anna received Jesus as her Lord and Savior. The kids and I were all sprawled out in the kitchen. I was sitting on the counter and the kids were standing around and sitting on the floor. Anna was sitting on a stepladder in front of my dangling legs. I'm not sure what brought it up, but we were talking about the reality of Heaven and Hell. All of a sudden (and very dramatically), Anna began to cry. I looked down at her, thinking she must have pinched herself in the step-ladder because it was so spontaneous, but after asking her what was wrong, it was obvious she wasn't hurt. Through her sobs she said, "God can't ever forgive me!" I kept thinking, *what could a six-year-old do that would cause God such displeasure,* but she was greatly conflicted in her spirit — and I suspect she understood God a little better than most children her age. Anna confessed that, after getting in trouble, she'd gone to the pantry and told God she hated Him. I was surprised she'd held God accountable the times she'd gotten in trouble. It didn't seem like something she'd do, but I assured her that God had no limitations in forgiveness. She believed me and wanted to be free from her guilt.

I took Anna to her room and sat with her on her bed. I reminded her that Jesus gave his life as a final sacrifice for our sins, and that He was calling her and asking her to allow Him to rescue her so she could be free once and for all. It took Anna a while (and reading more scripture) to realize that God really would forgive her, but eventually she believed me, believed God's word, and asked Jesus to become her Lord and Savior. She smiled from ear to ear and ran around the house telling her brothers and sisters that she was a Christian. She then called her daddy, who was out of town, and told him she became a Christian and wanted to be baptized. Of course Kyle was excited and told Anna he would baptize her just as soon as he could work it out.

While I was so blessed in my spirit, knowing that my

daughter had chosen to follow Jesus, I was also tormented in my heart because I felt as if Anna was preparing to leave this earth and I couldn't stand the thought of being without her. Anna's whole demeanor had changed and she had become very serious and thoughtful. She seemed to want to be by my side instead of playing. She was peaceful, but not radiating her normal lighthearted zeal for life.

I don't know if Kyle had the same concerns as I did, or if God was just prompting him without his knowing it, but one day he declared his plans to take us to Disneyland. The kids weren't just a little excited. We didn't have the money, but he was determined to figure out a way to get us there. "Life is short, let's go while we still can!" he said. Kyle understood that all too well.

Before actual plans were made, he mentioned our trip to Anna's heart doctor. The doctor said, "Well, you know, she would qualify for a Make-A-Wish trip" (and of course Anna would definitely make *that* wish). I mistakenly thought that he was telling me she was dying. I don't know if he read my worried expression or just clarified by accident, but he said that she would qualify because she had a life-*threatening* illness — a clarification that gave me great relief.

*****

We boarded a plane on November 2, 2004, to go see Mickey Mouse — well, perhaps Cinderella might be more accurate in this case! We weren't being sent to Disneyland in Annaheim, California, because the Make-A-Wish foundation worked with Give Kids the World and it was in Orlando, Florida. That was fine with us. We all looked forward to time away — someplace fun where we could clear our minds of all things stressful and just enjoy each other.

Anna had an awkward oxygen set-up and didn't travel very comfortably on the way there, but that improved on the way home when she was offered a little mask instead of nose tubes that were made for an adult, not a six-year-old.

There we were on the plane — all 10 of us! We were very happy to have my parents along (not to mention the blessing it was going to be to have two extra sets of hands to help with the little people). We were scattered here and there on the commercial jet. I sat by Anna and carried Jonas — the perfect little traveler — on my lap.

When we exited the plane, we laughed at ourselves for wearing sweaters and hoodies. It was hot and humid and we couldn't wait to shed our heavy clothing. When we got to Give Kids the World, we were tired but very excited. It was a colorful land of fantasy. We spent six days there being pampered, spoiled and abundantly fed. Everything was free, even the tempting ice cream parlor. The guys ordered banana splits while the rest of us tried to eat a little lighter. The staff at the resort treated Anna differently than the other kids and she didn't seem to like it. Their job was to give Anna the time of her life and they only meant well, but being one of many children, she wasn't used to special treatment. She never said so, but I'm pretty sure she felt bad that she was getting the nicer gifts and more attention. I also suspect she wondered deep in her heart why she was getting special treatment. For six years she had just been one of the Kraft kids and now, everywhere she went, she was the center of attention. She was put in the front of lines at the amusement parks and was personally greeted almost everywhere she went. She was a very smart child and I think she put two and two together and knew it was because she was sick.

Anna treated us all with special care during that trip. Not many six-year-olds would even think to do it, but she made sure she took turns riding in the van next to each one of us. She also rotated us on the rides. If she rode with me on one ride, she'd make sure she rode with Daddy on the next. She worked her way through every family member. It was as though she was carefully considering her last days. I don't think the rest of the family noticed, but besides being Anna's primary caretaker, I was her momma and only a mother and child can truly understand that bond. It was as though we were connected at the soul. As much as I resisted, I believe God was attempting to prepare my heart for Anna to leave me ... to live away from me and with her Savior ... except I don't think it's really possible to prepare for something so painful.

*****

We returned home from Anna's weeklong Disney trip on November 9. It was kind of sad to have to come back to reality, but a part of me was glad to be home. No more being spoiled, we were back to cooking and cleaning and carrying on as usual ... except Anna's health still wasn't improving and I wasn't at all myself because of it. I would have given anything to get back to the routine if we could have had Anna's health back as well.

We didn't have a set day, but unlike most Americans, we usually put up our Christmas tree before Thanksgiving. On November 17, Kyle was out of town but the kids were begging for the tree to go up! Even though Kyle's part of putting up the tree was merely sitting on the couch with Jared, drinking eggnog and watching *It's a Wonderful Life,* I was inclined to say "no." I wanted to wait for Kyle, but they made me call and ask him. Surprisingly, he said yes! I know now that God was communicating with him to allow us to put it up without him.

When Kyle came home on the 18th, the little kids ran to him and pulled him into the living room to see their beautiful work. They were pretty proud of themselves. That evening we had a wonderful time playing games, reading the Bible and listening to Christmas music around the tree. I really don't think it could have been any better. My heavy heart was consoled, but still, there was something tugging at it. We went to bed at a decent hour with everybody full of hugs, kisses and prayers. After crawling into bed, I picked up my journal and wrote, "Life is very sweet. I've had my moments when I despair and worry, but God always reminds me to count it all joy. Live today, today. After all, God's grace is sufficient and He may take us to our eternal home at any moment!" God reminded me that night that whether through life or death, his grace has the ability to carry us. He wanted me to understand that life was to be lived joyfully, one day at a time. When I went to sleep, my heart was at peace being reminded of that. I woke up about five hours later. It was 3:00 am. Anna was screaming.

Waking up to Anna's screams was becoming a familiar occurrence. It had been happening almost every night for the past few weeks. When I'd go check on her, she would usually be back to sleep already, but this night she was awake and sitting up. When I got to her bed, I was slightly frantic and asked, "What's wrong?"

"I don't feel well and I do *not* know why," Anna replied, with a lot of expression and maybe a little bit of fear too. I could tell she was going to throw up, so I picked her up and ran with her to the bathroom. As soon as I got her to the toilet, she vomited very violently and then just crumpled from the energy it took from her. I held her for a moment, then asked if she wanted to take a bath. The warm water of the tub is something I often use therapeutically for me, and my children.

While Anna soaked in the tub, we talked for a while. Since Christmas was approaching, we talked about presents and other related things. I could tell she didn't feel well, but the conversation seemed to be a distraction for a little while. When she had to throw up again, I put an empty yogurt container in front of her mouth. It was what I used to wash the kids hair. After she threw up, she decided she didn't want to be in the tub anymore, so I got her out, dressed her in her bright pink Winnie-the-Pooh shirt and some soft cotton pants and put her back in her bed.

Her heart was beating so hard and fast that she couldn't breathe well lying down, so I propped myself up on some pillows and laid her in front of me. I stroked her hair and gently touched her cheeks to provide her with some motherly comfort, but I also did it to comfort my own fearful heart. I desperately wanted Anna to be okay and for all of the frightening episodes to cease. I wondered how much more I'd have to endure as a mother.

As we lay there together, I could feel Anna's pounding heart slow down a bit. It brought me much comfort, as did her saying, "I feel so much better now." I let those words soothe me, but I'll admit I wasn't completely at peace. My mind was racing with questions. For days, I'd been brainstorming things I could do to help Anna. I'd done Internet research to find natural supplements to help her heart function better. Per her doctor's instructions, I had been giving her a baby aspirin a day to keep her blood thin. I was looking for something natural to add to that to maintain good circulation. I was desperate, knowing it wasn't the flu or a vitamin deficiency I was trying to cure, it was a heart defect, something impossible for me to ever fix and a problem too big to be resolved with home remedies. I was terrified as I realized I was losing control. I tried to shut out those thoughts but couldn't seem to do it. Distressed, yet hopeful, we lay there together for about 20 minutes until Jonas woke up in my bedroom.

I propped Anna up on some pillows for a minute and went in to Jonas. It was around 5:00 am and Kyle was just waking up to get ready for work. I asked him if he could bring Anna into the room. He picked her up, snuggled her against him and said, "So, you're not feeling well, huh?" She shook her head. He laid her down in his place on the bed and covered her up. I quickly went into the bathroom to get a cup in case she had to throw up, then I crawled back into bed with her and Jonas.

Anna seemed to be doing better and was very peaceful while I nursed Jonas. It was somewhat comforting to be snuggled up with my one-year-old while he nursed. I looked over at Anna a few times just to make sure she was breathing comfortably. She appeared to be comfortable, but it wasn't long before she screamed out and quickly sat up. She was panicked and fearful and continued to scream. I tried to calm her, but she was completely focused on whatever it was that was causing her pain. I begged her to stop. "Anna! You're going to hurt yourself!" Stop screaming! Anna, I'm serious! Stop it!" I was horrified and think I screamed back at her because of my own fear. I tried to communicate with her to no avail. She began to heave, so I grabbed the cup and she threw up in it. At that point she fell back on the bed. It was as if somebody slammed her down. I was afraid she'd vomit again and choke on it in that position. I tried to set her up, but it was as if her muscles were locked. She wouldn't move at all. As hard as I tried, I couldn't lift her. It was dark in the room so I couldn't see her expression — it would have helped me to better understand what she was feeling.

I quickly laid Jonas on the bed, switched on the light and yelled for Kyle. I couldn't get myself to leave the room so I continued to scream as loudly as I could. Eventually, he came running out of the bathroom, looking at me questioning and with fear on his face. I said, "Something's wrong with Anna! Call 911!" He ran to get the phone out of Jared's room, which of course woke Jared up, then ran back in while dialing. Jared came in and saw Anna lying on our bed stiff, blue and unresponsive. I glanced over at him and my heart instantly hurt. I didn't want him to suffer again. I hated that he'd seen so much in his life. Why did life have to be so unfair? It must have scared him to death to see Anna in such an unnatural state. Kyle said, "Go back to your room and pray, Jared. Pray really hard."

We automatically went through the motions of CPR, almost unaware of what we were doing. We had been trained for it — actually when Anna was born — but I'm surprised we remembered how to do it. I can only hope we did it right, and

I'm still not sure if we did. Instinctively, Kyle did the chest compressions and I breathed into Anna's mouth when it was my turn. Kyle also spoke to the 911 dispatcher. Everything seemed to take forever. Not knowing if Anna was feeling pain or any kind of emotion, I spoke to her and sang to her and assured her that Jesus was with her. I have a feeling she knew that better than I did.

Kyle's first words on the phone were, "I have an emergency!" and then proceeded to give out our address and phone number. I know those details are extremely important for the dispatcher to have, but it just seemed to take up precious time. We were desperately wanting and needing help. I didn't want the responsibility of trying to keep Anna alive; I didn't know how. I heard Kyle desperately say, "My daughter's sick and her heart just stopped!"

Between sobs and begging Anna to hang on, Kyle spoke with the 911 dispatcher. I was completely unaware of whether the person on the other end of the phone was a man or a woman, and I never asked. I just knew that I wanted the ambulance there as soon as possible and each second felt like an eternity.

I stayed right next to Anna's side the whole time. To my surprise, I was very quiet. I remember talking to Anna, singing to her, and using a very soft voice when speaking to her and to Kyle. I was completely beside myself with fear and I know I was in shock. Every anxiety I'd had in the previous months was playing out right before my eyes. The months of worry and dread were becoming reality. I had a strange calmness and a tremendous amount of fear all at the same time. I found myself thinking … *Is this Anna's time? Oh please, Lord, don't take Anna.* Even though I feared that very thing, I had never allowed myself to play it out in my mind.

Kyle continued to plead with the dispatcher. "Can they not find us? Do they need directions?" Through sobs he pleaded with Anna, "Come on, Honey. Hang on, Anna. I love you, Sweetheart." And he pleaded with the Lord, "Oh Lord, please. Oh Lord, please. Come on, Lord, please help her."

Anna's heart started and stopped several times, but there was a point when her eyes moved away from us. She no longer looked in our direction and we couldn't get her heart to start beating after that. Perhaps she saw something infinitely more dear on the other side. Was it the angels coming to take her to Jesus? I think that's the only thing that would have drawn her attention away from her mommy and daddy. Something in my heart ached and told me she was no longer dwelling in that precious body I'd held so many times and adored so dearly.

It took way too long for the ambulance to arrive! It had been 14 minutes since Kyle had made the phone call — the longest 14 minutes of my entire life. When they did finally show up, Jared went downstairs to let them in. A man came running up the stairs, started to do CPR, and then threw Anna over his shoulder and ran down the stairs with her. I don't remember him communicating with us, although he may have. I just remember watching him run down the stairs with my daughter dangled over his shoulder, and I hated it. I wanted him to fix her in front of me. I wanted to see her revive. I desperately wanted to communicate with her.

When he took her away, I felt totally helpless. At least when we were doing CPR we were doing something. Now we were alone with nothing to do. My heart yearned to be with my precious child. I didn't want Anna to be alone with strangers. They didn't know her. They didn't love her. My only consolation was that they had equipment that might help her.

We ran out and I began to crawl into the ambulance. They told me that I needed to stay out so I watched them from just outside the door. I was completely numb and couldn't even think. My entire body was trembling.

It didn't look like they were having any more luck than we were, but I was still hopeful. Kyle ran in to finish getting dressed and to tell Jared he would need to watch Jonas while we followed the ambulance to the hospital. I hated that for Jared; I absolutely hated it. Once again, I would have to abandon one child to be with another. It was pure torture, but there was nothing else I could do. I called my mom and dad on the way to the hospital and they were very soon on their way to be with Jared.

When we got to the hospital, I was asked to go to the front desk to give them information. Those mundane details seemed so unimportant at the time. I couldn't understand why it couldn't wait. I was asked simple questions. "What's your name? What's your address? What is your daughter's date of birth?" While they were simple questions, the answers didn't come. My voice was unsteady and my body shook, but somehow I managed to pull the answers out of my confused head.

When I got back to Kyle and Anna, I realized that she still wasn't breathing. I knew we had run out of hope. I just stood there next to Kyle, not saying anything. I'm not sure if any tears had even come yet. If they had, I don't remember. It was horrible watching the emergency staff work on our daughter, especially because her precious little body wouldn't respond. My heart told me she was gone. God spoke to my heart and told me that Anna was safe with Him.

At that point Kyle said, "If she's not coming back, we'd like to be able to say goodbye." I think that surprised them. It kind of surprised me, but he was right, we needed to be able to go to our daughter. Our hands needed to touch her and stroke her and … say goodbye to her.

*****

My mom had begun calling friends and before we knew it, we had three families by our side. Kyle was worried about Jared and called to tell him that Anna had died. Jared told him that he knew. I felt desperate for Jared. Our 14-year-old son was at home grieving alone. I knew I needed to get to him. I needed to hug him and tell him we would be okay. I desperately wanted him to know that, even though I didn't yet believe it.

My friend Renee knew I didn't want to leave Anna there alone, so she stayed with her at the hospital while Kyle and I went home to mourn with our family. Telling the children that Anna was gone, that she wouldn't be coming home, was horrible. Kyle explained it quickly: "Anna got very sick last night and this morning she went to be with Jesus." Cecily and Abigail were in shock. After it registered, Abigail's whole countenance fell and without moving her head or body at all, tears began to pour out of her eyes and she just sat there and cried. Cecily jumped out of her seat and ran up the stairs, sobbing loudly, but Kyle ran after her and held her very tightly. She wept so bitterly, I'll never forget it. I hated that she'd lost her best friend in life.

We attempted to comfort our precious children, but we had nothing to offer them other than our arms. We had no encouraging words for them ... only tears to cry with them. All of our hearts were desperate and broken. While we weren't without hope, it felt very close to that.

CHAPTER 8

It was a routine morning at work. There hadn't been many calls and I think my partner was off grabbing a cup of coffee. I was alone in the room when I got a call. It was 5:15 am. I said my usual, "911 Dispatch," but when the male voice on the other end said frantically, "Hello! I've got an emergency," I somehow knew it was a medical emergency. After asking him the questions necessary for dispatching the ambulance to the correct location, I proceeded with, "Okay, tell me what's going on. Tell me exactly what happened." That is the initial response we give once we establish that it is a medical call. The man's reply was actually shocking to me. He said, "My daughter's sick and her heart just stopped!" I responded with, "Her heart stopped? Is she breathing right now?" He was very scared and didn't respond to my question, but instead said, "She has heart problems!" I repeated my question, "Is she breathing?" He asked his wife if she was breathing and then quickly said, "She's barely breathing."

It's common to respond to such calls with a physiological reaction. I think a lot of dispatchers have the same initial physical response to emergency calls. This phone call was no exception. I became very hot, physically uncomfortable and irritable. I had a hard time focusing. My hands began to shake and I feared that, as soon as I began to talk, my voice would quiver. My breathing became shallow and rapid and without the ability to suppress it, I began to tear up. After I got through this series of physical responses, I felt queasy.

Everyday life doesn't hold these kinds of events, and though I, as a dispatcher, am trained to deal with them, it's still not natural.

Every single call we take — from routine to tragic — is unique. No two domestic disturbances are exactly the same, as are no two cardiac arrest calls. There are many variables in all situations — some we control and some we don't. Training provides an element of learning, but experience is the best teacher.

After the initial shock of the situation, I forced myself to think clearly and moved to paging out the ambulance. These initial moments are purely adrenaline-based. There isn't time to process emotion. I wasn't anxious to get back on the phone, knowing what would be required of me. It was the next step in the process, however, so I once again began to communicate with this fearful man who appeared on our caller I.D. screen as Kyle Kraft.

"Okay, sir, I do have them paged out. What's her status now?" I heard his daughter making noises. I asked, "Is that her I hear?"

"Yes, that's her right there. I have a faint heartbeat. We're doing CPR."

"You *are* doing CPR?"

He responded with a little relief in his voice. "Yeah, I got a little bit of a heartbeat."

At that moment I felt hopeful for the family. "Is she breathing on her own?" I was surprised when he said no.

"My wife's still giving CPR."

"Okay, about how old is your daughter?"

"She's six."

I had suspected she was young, but it's never easy to confirm that the emergency is for a child.

"Six years old," I repeated. "What condition does she have?"

"She has Heterotaxia — and a two-chambered heart."

I asked if this had ever happened before. His answer was very rushed, as if he was tired of small-talk.

"No sir. She's had a closed-heart surgery and two open-heart surgeries. We need to get somebody here quick!"

I assured him that they were coming as quickly as they could and that I would remain on the phone with him. I heard his daughter making noises in the background again, then him say to her, "Come on, Sweetie."

I told him that he could set the phone down if he needed to help with the CPR and he told me that he was doing chest compressions while his wife was breathing into her. I could hear his daughter making more noises and her dad began to sob and say to her, "Oh, Honey. Come on. Come on." He then said to me, "I think her heart stopped again."

I could hear her and asked, "Is she breathing at all on her own because I can hear her making sounds."

He was crying when he said, "It sounds like she has some sort of obstruction."

"Did she choke on anything?" Panicked, he said, "No! She didn't! She was sick! She was throwing up!" I heard he and his wife discussing readjusting some pillows and I told them that it would be good to get everything out from underneath her. He then told me that he thought she was breathing a little on her own. I heard him say to his daughter, "That's a good girl, Hannah. Keep breathing, Honey. Pray for Jesus to help you, Honey. That's a girl. Ah, good girl. That's right. They're coming to help. Just hold on."

I was shocked when I heard him say "Hannah," my daughter's name. I immediately thought of my own little girl, just a few years younger than this man's daughter. Somehow my own love for my daughter was thrown into the emotional mix and my brain began to make connections between my deepest love for my daughter and this little girl I didn't know. Her daddy was encouraging her and I could hear her faintly. She seemed to be hanging in there and her daddy seemed to be somewhat peaceful. I was grateful for the short moment to deal with the emotions that had overtaken me. I was also very drawn into the intimacy of this call, especially when I heard him tell his daughter "Pray for Jesus to help you." They shared something that I didn't fully understand.

I then heard her dad say, "Keep praying, Jared. I think it's working, Honey." I didn't know who Jared was, but I assumed it was his son. Then I heard him say to his daughter, "There you go. That's my sweetie."

I asked him if they were still doing CPR and he said, "She's on her own now."

"Okay, good." And I meant those words. I kept my voice calm, but I felt greatly relieved over this and was hoping she would only improve at this point.

I then heard Kyle say under his breath, "Oh my gosh." I sensed he was becoming overwhelmed and spoke again to distract him, "Does she seem to be improving as time goes by a little bit or not?"

He asked his wife, "Is she improving, Honey," then he said to me, "Barely — we need to get somebody here soon."

"Yeah, yeah." Before I could say anything else I heard him talking to his daughter. "Hang in there, Hannah. That's right. Just hang in there, Sweetie."

Then to me he said, "She's having a hard time breathing."

I told him that if she was breathing a little on her own, she might do better on her side. I could hear he and his wife adjusting her position. I heard him talking to his wife, "Honey, I'm going to take Jo Jo to Jared, okay?" I could only assume that Jo Jo was yet another child in the room. I could picture the sad scene and hated it for them.

I asked the man what had led up to the incident and he

told me his daughter had been sick for a couple of hours —
that she had been vomiting. When I said, "Okay," he asked
me if that was a symptom of something. I could tell he was
just desperate and wanting help — any help at all. I explained
that I just needed to let the EMS know all the details that I
could to help them do a better job when they got there.

At this point, his daughter began to make a lot of noise
and I could tell they had started CPR again.

"Let Momma help you breathe, Honey."

I asked if she was breathing on her own and he responded
with, "Not right now, and no heartbeat! There you go. Hang
in there, Hannah. Jesus is with you, Honey. Let's get that
heart going again." She continued to make noise and he said
pleadingly, "Come on, Honey."

I asked if they were doing CPR again and while crying,
he said faintly, "Yeah. Where are they?" His voice told me
he was beginning to lose hope. I was beginning to hate
this phone call. I had entered an emotional level I wasn't
comfortable with. I could only think of my own little girl and
what this poor family must be suffering. I assured the man
that they were coming. He began to cry more and seemed to
be giving up.

"Come on, Hannah. Let's get that heart going. Lord,
please! Come on, Lord. *Please,* Lord, *help* her!"

I wasn't sure how much longer I could stand hearing his
desperate pleas. I felt utterly helpless. He was so sad when
he said, "She's so little," and that's what I was thinking too.

I took a few more moments to brief the ambulance, and when I got back on the phone, I asked how she was doing. He sobbed and said, "She's not doing well. She's not doing well at all. Can they not find us? Do they need directions?" I told him that they were almost there, but I'm sure he didn't believe me. It had been too long. We both knew that.

I asked some more questions about her heartbeat and her pulse. He confirmed that there was no pulse and that they were still doing CPR. I tried to comfort him a little by saying, "You're doing real good with her," but I knew there wasn't any real comfort in that.

I told him that I thought the ambulance was on their street and asked him if they had a porch light. They didn't, but he told his son to go turn on house lights and unlock the door. Between sobs, "Hannah, I love you, Sweetheart."

I heard her making noise, then heard him say, "Come on, Sweetie."

He then said to me, "I don't hear a siren. They don't have their siren on or what?"

I told him that I thought they had been held up by a train and were trying to go around. I told him to hang on and I'd check with them. When I got back on the line, I told him they were clear of the train and almost there. I asked how the situation was.

"Same. No heartbeat." I encouraged him to just keep going with it. He was worried. "It's been too long."

I was afraid he was right.

"Come on, Baby. Come on." Kyle let out a loud cry and then continued, "Come on Sweetie, come on!" After confirming with him that her heart was not beating and that she was not breathing, I told him that the ambulance was there. He confirmed that they were.

"Okay, I'll let you go. Good luck."

He simply said, "Bye."

I sat for a moment in a daze. It was 5:29 am. I had spent 14 minutes on the phone — it was the longest emergency call I had ever been on. It was hard to process all that had happened, and I was sad … and numb.

CHAPTER 9

When somebody close to you dies, there's a tremendous amount of business to be dealt with. It's helpful in that it distracts a little from the intense emotional pain, but it's tedious and tiring as well. I'm not sure how everything got done, but Anna's casket was chosen (a pure white), her burial clothes were picked (a pink dress she'd worn for tea parties and dress-up), a plot at the cemetery was bought (near her big brothers), and the memorial service was planned (with a beautiful presentation of pictures and video that I stayed up 36 hours straight to complete).

The most painful time for me during my grief was the morning after Anna died. I was surprised I slept at all; I suppose it was from sheer exhaustion. I woke very early (around 4:00 am) with the most pitiful feeling of sadness in my heart. Anna's absence caused a real physical pain; it was as if my heart and body craved her heart and body. I wouldn't be exaggerating to say I felt as if I was wasting away from sorrow.

I looked over to Kyle, only to discover he wasn't in bed. I couldn't lie there by myself, so I went looking for him. The bathroom was locked, so I knocked on the door and Kyle opened it. I suppose my expression told him I needed help — his told me the same thing. He pulled me into the bathroom and pushed the door shut. I buried my head into his chest and we cried together. It wasn't a gentle cry, we cried from the depths of our souls, then dropped to the floor exhausted and wept some more. I remember saying, "I can't live without her. I can't. I'll never be happy again." Kyle couldn't console me because he felt the same way. I confessed to him, "I just want to die."

Kyle cried out, "Lord, just come and take us all to be with her."

We would have happily left the earth at that very moment, but only if our other children could go with us. We didn't want them to hurt anymore than they already were.

Those days following Anna's death were the longest, most painful days of my life. I was so heartbroken, I could barely function. I feel so guilty admitting it, but even though I loved and adored my other children every bit as much as I did Anna, they brought me little, if any, joy during my early days of grief. The pain was consuming and irrational. One saving force was that I hated watching them hurt, so I made every effort to hide my own pain and help them cope with theirs. I forced myself to tell them that we'd heal and be okay — even though I wasn't sure I believed it. It was my love for them that made me strive for happiness and restoration, even while I was too sad to feel any of that happiness.

*****

I struggled so much with guilt for the first few days. I would lie in bed, stare up at the ceiling, and envision clouds and empty spaces with Anna wandering alone, as if she was lonely and sad. I saw her searching for me, and I hated myself for abandoning her. My sick heart was telling me I didn't fight hard enough ... that I could have done something to save her ... but instead I let her slip away. Her arms reached to me and her eyes begged me to reach for her and pull her back to me, but I couldn't.

My spirit knew she didn't need me, but I couldn't convince my flesh of it. My arms had held her so many times and my lips had kissed her day after day. It was me who met most of her needs and now I could meet them no more. I felt as if I failed her in some way.

*****

Daily life seemed impossible. My family still had to eat and we needed things from the store that seemed so mundane and useless, even though they weren't. Nobody at the stores or the post office knew I was hurting. They didn't treat me any differently than anybody else, but I was different than everybody else. When cashiers were rude, I wanted to beg them to treat me carefully, and at the same time yell at them. The only people I wanted in my life were those I knew really loved me and cared for me. I especially desired the company of those who loved Anna.

We were accused of not reacting with enough sadness the morning Anna died (that individual apparently had never experienced shock). We heard rumors of comments such as, "Do you think Anna would still be alive if Lynnette had called 911 when Anna first got sick?" If that person only knew the guilt I struggled with already. We also heard, "Well, at least they knew Anna was sick. It probably made it easier." Easier? Can anything make the loss of your child easier?

One lady at Sam's Club said that I must have been tempted to love Anna at "arm's length" since I knew she might die someday. In my pain and with no strength to fight off the evil thoughts, I had a tendency to wish they could feel the pain I was feeling — for just one day. I just didn't understand why people couldn't keep thoughts to themselves when those thoughts were so coldhearted.

People usually aren't intentionally cruel, but I don't think any grieving person has the ability to cope with such careless remarks. If anybody should put forth extra effort to do and say the right thing, it should be those who are in the support role, not those who are used up by grief.

CHAPTER 10

I got off the phone with Kyle and just sat there in a sort of shock. I wasn't entirely aware of what was going on around me. My partner was likely sitting there next to me, but I didn't notice. Having been on the job for many years, she'd experienced just about every type of call. I guess she knew I needed time to process the call and recover from the emotional impact it had made. She didn't ask me any questions.

It was 5:30 am and I couldn't leave until 8:00 am. Thank goodness the calls I took after that were routine and didn't require much of me. There was one phone call I hoped I wouldn't have to take. It came at 6:32 am. It was the chaplain from the hospital requesting a call from the coroner. I didn't ask, but knew that call was regarding Kyle's daughter. While I had nearly given up hope that Hannah would live, I still wanted to witness a miracle. When that phone call came, I knew the little girl had died. There was no more hoping, she was gone. I felt so sad. I'd come to know this little girl on the phone as Hannah, so how could I not personalize that pain. What if it had been my little Hannah?

I grieved for this man and his family, and somehow I grieved for myself, although I wasn't sure what all of that was about.

When my shift finally ended and I walked out to my truck, I was struck with the feeling that everything should be different, but it wasn't. Everything was exactly the same as it had been before the call. Nobody around me knew about this family. The call that crushed me didn't mean anything to anybody else. Somehow, I had to get in the truck and go home.

The short drive home seemed to take forever. I was barely aware of what I was doing. I just couldn't shake the feeling of emptiness. Why did my heart feel lonely for a little girl I'd never spent a moment with? After weeping all the way home, I walked into a quiet house. I was alone.

I knew I wouldn't be able to sleep right away, so I tried to drown out my thoughts with my headphones. Despite the loud music pounding in my ears, I couldn't help but replay that call in my head. Over and over again, I tried to analyze it. I couldn't think of anything I could have done differently — I'd never learned anything about a child with heart problems going into cardiac arrest — but I still felt guilty. The only calls I'd ever taken with a child in cardiac arrest were related to choking or drowning, and it was common for those children to survive. I just couldn't shake the feeling that I might have been able to save that little girl.

I was physically exhausted and emotionally spent. As I

lay down to try to rest, I thought about how devastated Kyle and his family must be. I came home to a peaceful house and they went home to grieve. My family wasn't suffering. Their family, on the other hand, was experiencing something I knew nothing about.

I wondered what had happened after I got off the phone with Kyle. I knew they would have followed the ambulance to the hospital, but I thought about those children who had been in the room when the call was made. Where were they? How were they coping with the loss of their sister?

There were so many unanswered questions going through my mind. Would they be able to go on? How long does it take to recover from something like that? I couldn't imagine life without Taylor or Hannah, and the thought made me grieve for Kyle and his family even more. I prayed for them because it was all I knew to do, but I doubted my prayers were being heard.

It took effort going back to dispatch that night. I had barely slept and I was still filled with that empty feeling I was beginning to recognize as depression. I was mixed with two very prominent emotions — sadness and guilt. Kyle's voice tormented me. I couldn't get his cries and pleas out of my head. There was so much fear … so much grief. I just couldn't help but wish I could have spared him that pain.

When I walked back into work that night, things were pretty much as usual. It was becoming painfully obvious that I was the only one who was affected by that call. Somehow

I felt that the world had changed in those 14 minutes, but it had only changed for me.

My co-workers had all experienced their own difficult calls. That comforted me. We had a bond that not many would understand. I didn't need to explain anything to them, they just knew I was trying to cope. I'm sure they had faith I would bounce back like they had all done before, but I was troubled by just how much I was affected. I was concerned I wouldn't bounce back.

This little girl's death was at the forefront of my mind and I was profoundly sad. My general sense of guilt became finely focused that day at a meeting when I was directly blamed for her death. I was told that if I would have counseled Kyle differently, his daughter would be alive. To me, this was confirmation that what I had been feeling was, in fact, the truth.

Those words destroyed me. It took my depression to a new level. I felt I had killed a six-year-old little girl, and not just any little girl, but the one who belonged to this man who had begged me to help him, this man who begged Jesus to save his daughter and expressed his heart of love so freely that I couldn't get his words out of my head. His daughter was gone and now it was confirmed — I could have prevented it.

CHAPTER 11

Anna was everywhere — in my conscious thoughts and in my dreams. Night after night she either made an appearance in a dream or completely overtook it. When I'd have a pleasant dream about her, I'd wake up so disappointed to discover it wasn't real. Yet, I was also strangely satisfied because it was as though she visited me while I was sleeping.

One night I dreamed that Anna had come back from Heaven; I saw her walk into the room. I picked her up, not believing how her touch warmed me and made my heart come to life. With tenderness and passion, I said to her, "Oh Anna! I love you! I've missed you so much!" As I held her very tightly, yet also gently, I asked in an almost begging tone, "Can you please stay with me?" She started to nod her head and I rejoiced in my heart that I would have her back in my life, but then she turned sad and began to slowly shake her head. It was as if she wished she could stay but knew it was impossible.

She gently looked into my eyes and comforted me by saying so sweetly, "No, Momma, but I'll see you again." Anna's voice held such encouragement and hope. While I should have been devastated at the realization that she couldn't stay, I somehow felt a sense of peace because I believed her. I believed we'd be together again.

For many days — perhaps even weeks — I dreamed about Anna almost every night. Not all the dreams were comforting; some were torture. One time I dreamed that I had abandoned Anna and Silas to ride a rollercoaster. When I was on the ride, I realized I had left them and panicked. I made them stop the ride so I could get off. I began running, frantically looking for them, but my feet wouldn't move fast enough, like they were too heavy to move. I woke up before I ever found them and felt so hopeless. I wondered if my feeling of guilt over Anna's death had caused that dream.

On another night I dreamed that Cecily was dying. I was trying to make it easier for both of us by telling her that she was going to get to be with Anna. I woke up so upset — yet relieved — when I realized Cecily was alive and well. Death had affected me so severely that I feared it. I saw it everywhere — even in life. Though my heart knew the truth — that Anna had gained something infinitely more dear when she died — I couldn't see it from that perspective … her perspective. I could only see it from mine and it hurt. It hurt like nothing ever had. I hated it. Death was my enemy. Through moments of joy in seeing Anna again, to desperate dreams of loss and painful awakenings, I grieved.

*****

Every little thing took more effort than I wanted to give it. Even eating was too much work. My mom had to bring food to me and force me to eat. My mouth didn't want to chew. It all tasted the same; even the food that usually tempted me had no appeal at all.

I didn't care what I was wearing or how I looked. If I hadn't had children to care for, I'm not sure I would have been able to get out of bed. My only motivation was for them. I didn't want to socialize, I hated answering the phone, I hated making small talk. The only people I wanted to talk to were people who were hurting with me, or were close to me. I wanted people to feel sorry for me. I wanted people to know I was wounded. I sat down one day to write a letter to a friend who lived out of town and I poured my heart out to her. I described my life as lonely and told her I didn't think I'd ever recover. I let my tears drip on the paper on purpose as proof of how desperate and lonely I was.

I didn't want people to ignore my tragedy. So many people tried to do that. I remember running into a lady who I hadn't seen in a long time. I knew she had heard about our loss, but she didn't even say, "I'm sorry." She just went on and on about her life and her kids and didn't even acknowledge my pain. I hadn't spent a lot of time with her, so I wasn't really surprised at her lack of concern, but that conversation made me wish I'd never have to see her again. How could she carry on as if my loss was insignificant? People who are suffering need love. Those who are grieving need support. To disregard someone's pain is to say, "I don't care."

One day a call came with an invitation to a Christmas party. I felt a little angry about it at first. I'd never been much of big event person anyway, but socializing in any form had become very unappealing. My first inclination was to decline — in fact I did at first — but the invitation had come from a friend who did care and I knew she was hoping to provide some relief and fun for us. I was reminded by my mom that this was her way of reaching out to our family and that we should consider going. I knew she was right, but I was so self-absorbed that I didn't think it was fair that I should be expected to go. We weren't in the mood to celebrate — not even our Savior's birth. I knew Jesus understood.

One reason I feared going to this particular party was because this friend had a daughter Anna's age; a daughter who had been Anna's friend. Seeing little girls was so hard for me. It didn't matter if she had red hair, blue eyes and a thin, freckled face instead of Anna's brown hair, brown eyes and full face. If there was a little girl, she reminded me of my little girl and I wanted mine back.

It seemed so unfair to me when I saw a lady sitting in church one day with her three little girls snuggled up against her. It made me want my three little girls snuggled up next to me. I became jealous. Why was she allowed to keep hers and I wasn't allowed to keep mine? Why did God keep taking my children?

*****

Kyle and I celebrated our 16th wedding anniversary on December 17, even though we didn't feel much like celebrating at all. Instead of staying home to sulk, we went out to do it. I think we hoped a night away might provide an escape or maybe even just some numb time. We got dressed up, wondering if playing the part might help make the night a success. When I put my skirt on, I realized I had lost a significant amount of weight.

Kyle bought me a new camera for Christmas and had given it to me early, so Abigail took pictures of us with it before we left. I wanted to be cheerful and wished I could smile sincerely, but every time we made new memories, I ached inside. I didn't want to make new memories. I felt I was betraying Anna.

Kyle and I left the house with smiles on our faces, hoping the kids wouldn't see our pain. We drove to the show, barely saying anything, which was not like us at all. We parked in a small, dark parking lot and made our way into the theater. We were escorted by the hostess, glad to be seated close to the stage. We hoped sitting close would keep us awake and help us enjoy the show. The buffet wouldn't open for about 30 minutes. Neither of us was in the mood to talk, so we just sat there, boredom taking over.

We were very glad when the buffet opened because it gave us something to do. While we ate, we visited a little but it was then that I realized it had been a mistake to leave home. I missed the kids and I was tired. I just wanted to snuggle with Jonas and go to sleep. Kyle didn't seem to be enjoying himself either. When the show finally started, we tolerated it until the intermission — I had literally dropped my head to the table on several occasions and dozed off — so we left.

CHAPTER 12

What is it that makes a person prone to depression? Why had I been cursed with the tendency to feel things so deeply? I couldn't shake it, I couldn't pull myself out of the sad state I was in. I had no defenses against the conviction I felt over my failure to protect the little girl who had died. While I wasn't convinced that I could have done anything differently, I couldn't help feeling that I might have saved her life.

Jo spent time listening to me and really tried to understand my depression. I did appreciate her efforts, but how can a man convince his wife he should be grieving so deeply over another man's daughter – one he didn't even know? It wasn't natural and caught me by surprise too. Jo had her own emotional connections at work dealing with the occasional loss of a baby, but she wasn't prone to depression as I was. She quietly grieved over those babies and for those parents, but never sought words of comfort from me. Sadly, she knew I had nothing to offer her. She wasn't emotionally sick like I was. Unlike Jo, I was a slave to my emotions.

As usual, my pain made me retreat to a world of diversions.

I used every resource available — especially music — to send my mind to other places. While the music pounded in my ears, Kyle's voice invaded as well. My mind was confused … chaotic. There was no peace, but there was a certain amount of satisfaction in embracing the pain because I felt I deserved it.

Sleep didn't come easily over the next few days. I couldn't shut down. Closing my eyes only made visions of death clearer. I was entirely distracted by the images of Kyle, his wife and his little girl. I imagined them hating me for letting them down, but there was absolutely nothing I could do to change the situation. I would have done anything for them. Out of desperation I prayed for them, but still, no peace came. I believed there was a God, but I didn't understand God. Why did He allow horrible tragedies to happen? I prayed, but I didn't expect Him to answer. I didn't understand spiritual things.

I continued to go to work, but even when I was physically there, I wasn't really there at all. I had lost all confidence in myself. It was like being back in the early days of dispatch when every call I took made me nervous, only now I was actually terrified. I dreaded picking up the phone. I desperately feared another disaster … another death. My passion for my work was gone. The compassion that once existed for those I was on the phone with was gone. I considered giving up my job because I felt worthless. I couldn't break free from the debilitating thoughts that continually swam around my confused mind.

On my way to work one evening, I picked up a newspaper. I was so preoccupied with Hannah's death that I knew I had to see the obituary. I wasn't sure if it would be there, but I hoped it would be. I didn't open the paper when I first picked it up; I threw it beside me in my truck and continued on to work. I planned to wait until later that night, after things quieted down. I looked forward to it and dreaded it at the same time.

Later, when I had a moment to break away, I opened the paper. Breathing deeply, I slowly made my way to the obituaries. When it was in front of me, I let out a sigh. I hadn't expected a picture, but there she was, an adorable little dark-haired girl. For the first time, I was able to put a face to this six-year-old I was grieving. It caught me off guard and completely took my breath away, yet I think I was grateful for that picture. Another detail that surprised me was that her name wasn't Hannah after all. It was Anna ... Anna Gabrielle Kraft. The very detail that sucked me in so deeply wasn't even correct. I heard Hannah, and that's what drew me into this tragedy. Was I destined to grieve with this family?

As I continued to digest this newly discovered detail, I read the obituary through teary eyes. I was surprised to realize that Anna was one of six children ... *so many people to have to suffer ... so many people to experience such deep loss.* I also noticed that it wasn't Kyle and his wife Lynnette's first loss. They'd also lost two sons. I wondered about those boys — Samuel and Josiah. Were they twins? Had they also been born with sick hearts? This family's story — or what I knew of it — seemed so sad. I wondered if they were as depressed as I was. Surely, they must be. How could they not be?

For some reason, I decided I needed to keep the obituary near me. I took a pair of scissors and began cutting it out. As I cut, my sadness boiled over and by the time I was finished, I was sobbing. I took my headset off and threw it on the counter. I put my head down and rubbed my hand over my eyes. I then quickly stood up, picked up the paper, carried it to the break room and slammed it down on the table. I felt myself breaking down. I knew I needed to compose myself, so I left the dispatch center for a few minutes and walked around in the hallway. When I came back, my partner looked in my direction but didn't confront me. I took Anna's obituary and put it in my wallet. I wasn't sure why I had to keep it, but I did.

The next morning I anxiously waited outside my boss' office. When he came, I followed him inside. I rambled as I tried to explain to him that I thought I was losing it. I hoped he could help me understand why I couldn't get past the call that I took on November 19. I confessed my guilt over the situation. He sincerely wanted to help me and he tried to ease my mind, but as he attempted to console me, his words fell on deaf ears. I wanted to hear it but I wouldn't allow myself to be comforted.

When he realized his attempts were failing, he went

one step further and called the coroner to get more details about Anna's death. Later, he called me back to his office and told me I couldn't have done anything to prevent it. She had a sick heart and nothing could have been done to save her. I appreciated his efforts, and at that moment I respected him more than I ever had, but still, his words provided me no comfort. Seeking his help was useless. I was useless. Nobody could help me.

Over the next several weeks, I continued to struggle with depression. I remained buried in my music and consumed in tormenting thoughts. I was distant from everything and everybody except the one thing I wanted to be distanced from — Anna's death. My wife and parents questioned my sadness. I knew it was wrong to grieve like I was. I shouldn't have been so caught up in another's life, especially the life of a complete stranger. I couldn't explain it to anybody. I wished I could have, because then I might have been able to stop.

Many nights, when Jo was at work and I was with the kids, I would just hold Hannah and cry. It was comforting to have her in my arms, but I grieved Kyle's loss at the same time. I knew I appreciated Hannah's life more since the morning I took that dreadful call. I knew I was lucky to have my daughter. I wished I didn't feel guilty having been spared that sort of pain, but for some reason I did. Kyle's daughter should have been in his lap … but never would be again. Hannah asked me one night why I was so sad, but how do you explain death to a three-year-old? My heart knew that Anna's death and Hannah's life were somehow intertwined, but I couldn't figure out how. How was I going to escape the guilt and move on? How would my pain resolve itself? I held my daughter and let her touch comfort me. I began to hope a little, but in what I didn't know.

CHAPTER 13

Surviving those first few weeks was kind of like hanging on for dear life. God did give me peace when I was willing to receive it, but there were times when I didn't want it. Grieving was miserable, yet somehow felt satisfying at times. I hated it, yet I knew it was inevitable. I needed to cry and miss my daughter. The only way through it was *straight* through it. There was no avoiding the pain. If I held anything in, it would just have to come out later. I was so anxious to get past it that the last thing I wanted to do was prolong it.

I continued to journal through every thought, emotion and prayer, just as I had done when Anna was in the hospital. It was again a safe place to vent all of my irrational thoughts, but it became a beautiful way to watch God work in my heart and through my sorrow. As I penned my thoughts, I also began to look to God's word for comfort. The fog lifted enough so that I could see God at work, and as this happened, my spirit began to revive. God communicated with me by the most unusual means. I knew the God who created me was also hurting for me, and I knew He wanted to prove to me that He was right by my side willing to walk the horrible path of grief with me … and for me.

*****

Abigail and I set out to find the perfect little decorative pieces to grace the memorial room we were putting together for Anna. We went to Hobby Lobby, parting and going in opposite directions once inside. After Abigail walked away, I stood and stared at the store contents for a moment. I felt overwhelmed and so tired. Silently, I prayed, "Lord, please show me something that will comfort my heart and remind me of Anna."

Weary and full of self-pity, I took my cart and began searching for something … anything to remind me of Anna. As I roamed the aisles, I reminisced about Anna's likes, dislikes, talents and charms, and spotted a few things along the way that seemed appropriate for the room. As I moved slowly through the store, I also spotted an older couple near me several times. While I noticed them, I didn't think anything of it. You know how it is when you're in a store passing the same people in the aisles over and over again.

Abigail and I met up at some point and I realized she was more interested in looking at things that appealed to her — like scrapbooking items — but she was only 11 and I didn't expect her to be able to stay focused on the task. I ended up going all the way around the store. When I was back up at the front, I began looking at the silk flowers. As I turned the corner, I saw the same couple yet again. We had been in the store together for nearly an hour. I looked at them and began to teasingly say, "Are you guys following me?" But something stopped me. As I looked into their eyes, I saw something very sincere. It was as if they were looking into my heart. Instead of teasing, I simply smiled and said, "Hi." They were standing right next to each other, directly in front of me, not moving at all. I think they may have been holding hands. The lady smiled very sincerely but softly. In a very gentle tone they both said, "Hello." I felt as if their words embraced my spirit. I felt as if their eyes said, "I know you're hurting, but Jesus will heal you." I sensed something more than human kindness.

Each of them looked so soft and gentle. The man had gray hair and smooth-looking skin. He didn't smile but had a countenance of peacefulness. The woman had soft brown hair that was short and curled under at the chin. She had very fair skin and little round eyes.

We held each other's attention for another moment, and then in awkward silence I decided to move on. As I walked away, I realized that this couple that had been following me around for almost an hour had no cart and no merchandise. I don't even think the lady had a purse. I felt a strong sense that God had sent comforting spirits to help ease my pain in some way.

Abigail found me soon after that and we went through

the checkout. I floated out the door and experienced an overwhelming sense of awe. Regardless of who those people were, God used them to help me know that He was near me, watching every move I made. I think there was more to that couple. I think I had a divine encounter, and after I told Abigail about it in the car, she thought so too.

*****

We were all still deep in grief, but the kids were excited for Christmas. Their young hearts were looking for something to bring them joy, and the thought of Christmas presents did that. Although I still had shopping to do, I had picked up a few things that I could wrap up for them. I knew it was something that would make them smile and get their minds off of their broken hearts. What child doesn't love being handed a present, even if they're only allowed to manipulate it and shake it a bit until it's time to open it. I was happy to do that for them — I really was — but I also grieved as I wrapped. I wanted to wrap up a doll or a dress for Anna. Every time I wrote a name on a package, I was reminded that I wouldn't be writing Anna's name on any of them.

I sat on the floor of the bedroom, heavy-hearted but with determination. I would get through this task for my kids, even if it killed me. The bedroom I sat in had been Cecily's and Anna's room just a few short weeks before. After Anna died, we knew Cecily would move into a room with Abigail.

The memories of them together in that room threatened to move me to another room for wrapping, but Anna's memory was in the next room, too, as that was the bedroom she died in. There was no escaping — she had been everywhere in our home.

I decided to wrap a doll I'd picked out for Cecily. I always bought Cecily and Anna matching clothes and toys. If Anna had been alive, I certainly would have bought one for her too. I dropped my head, let out a deep sigh and just sat still for a moment. Like I'd done so many times before, I silently wondered why. Why did I have to lose another child? Why did I have to lose a child at all?

When I gained a little courage, I carried on by placing the package on the wrapping paper. I cut enough paper to fit around the box, then began to pull it up and around the gift. As I pulled one of the cut sides up to the other cut side, I noticed right away that the patterns from each side matched up perfectly. I just sat and stared for a moment, wondering how in the world I had managed to do that. It was not a simple pattern; it had the lyrics to *Silent Night* in jumbled form all over the paper.

Then God spoke to me. *Lynnette, you think that you have to manage your pain, but you don't. Let me carry your burden. Just as you cut the paper without giving it a second thought, I want you to walk through your grief without worrying about each moment of pain. My child, just as the paper pattern matched up without your knowledge or care, so will the grief work itself out without a single effort of your own. Just walk through this grief one step at a time and I will work out your healing. Everything will match up just as perfectly as the paper and it will all make sense to you one day. Just trust me.*

The message was loud and clear. God gave me great confidence at that moment. I knew I'd be okay. I knew that He was actively working in my sorrow and resolving all the conflicts of my heart. I gained a great deal of peace that night... and it was a lesson learned through something as simple as wrapping paper.

*****

We were bombarded with sympathy cards in the weeks after Anna died. Sometimes they made me cry, but I still appreciated receiving them because they told me people cared that we were suffering. There was often a letter from a friend expressing their sadness over our loss, and once in a while we'd receive a gift of some sort. I appreciated that support and looked forward to checking the mail each day.

One unseasonably warm day, I walked across the road to the mailbox, hoping I'd find something to make me feel better. Receiving a letter from a friend, I walked slowly back towards the house, sat on the bumper of our van and read it completely through. This friend had been reading a book about Hudson Taylor — missionary to China in the mid 1800s. She told me that he'd lost his seven-year-old daughter (Grace) to meningitis. I don't remember what she quoted in the letter, but I remember feeling immense sorrow for Hudson Taylor. I understood the pain he spoke of. He sounded desperate at his loss, just as I was. I found myself wondering why she sent the letter because nothing in it gave me a glimpse of hope at all. I could so easily relate to what it said and it made me so sad.

When I was done reading, I folded the letter up and put it back in the envelope. I didn't move. I wasn't ready to walk back to the house — not until I had recovered. I felt crushed in my spirit. I knew my friend was just trying to show me that she was sorry for me … that she knew I had that same sorrow, and I was grateful for that, but I wasn't the type of person that thrived on sad companionship. While there were times that I needed to be sad and I needed to be allowed to cry, I never sought out sad people so we could sulk together. I wasn't wired that way at all. I'd always been the type of person who looked for something helpful, something hopeful in all situations, and that letter didn't offer any of that.

Just moments later, God brought something unexpected to my mind. I suddenly came to the realization that Hudson Taylor was with his daughter, and it was then that I smiled. His waiting was over. His grief was gone. Like me, he had feared life without his daughter, but he no longer lived in that fear because he now lived with his daughter in Heaven. I was reminded that there would be a day when my grief would be over too. Completely. The hope of eternity was certain. Someday I would live with Anna again in Heaven and nobody could ever take that from me.

When I had that to lift my spirits, I was able to get up off the bumper and make my way back to the house and to my children. I had something to share with them that would likely lift their spirits too. Someday, we'd all be together again in Heaven and we'd never have to be sad again. The day I was reminded of that was the day Hudson Taylor's words were delivered to my mailbox. God's resources are unlimited and I find myself often amazed at what and who He uses to minister to my needs. I never would have expected that letter or that outcome.

CHAPTER 14

As much as I hoped I would just wake up one morning and my grief would be gone, it didn't happen that way. There were no magic words that removed my sadness or my guilt and there was no epiphany that released me from my depression. Time proved to be the best healer, and really the only healer for me. Anna's death wasn't ever far from my mind, but the raw emotions of it dulled over time. There were still times when I was at home in the middle of the night and would quietly mourn the little girl I never knew and never would know, but as my heart began to recover, those moments came less often.

After several weeks of sustained and intense depression and sadness, the routine of everyday life forced me to move on. Taylor was in the first grade and I was excited to get to see his first Christmas concert at school. Hannah was three and I spent many hours cooking with her in her play kitchen. Jo depended on me to help with the household, but also wanted me to be a supportive husband and good father. My roles at home were somewhat satisfying and there were many days that I laughed and was carefree, but I could never seem to stay in that peaceful place for long. My depression was a part of me as much as anything else was. I wished it would just disappear, but it wasn't something I had any control over.

Passion for my job was still absent, but I had a family to support, Christmas presents to buy and bills to pay. Regardless of what I hoped I could do instead of dispatching, I had no choice but to keep working. My family depended on me. I had years and years of experience putting one foot in front of the other in the midst of depression, and that's what I had to continue to do. So, day after day, I went to work.

*****

Earlier in the year, one of my co-workers at dispatch had the opportunity to receive specialized training in what was called "tactical dispatching." He thought this concept would be a valuable addition to our center and to our local SWAT team. He discussed the program with our boss and eventually convinced him and the SWAT team commander that we needed to start a special program that would put specially trained dispatchers out into the field on SWAT calls. This team would assist with on-scene communications. I was chosen to work with him as the program was established. I was excited to have an opportunity to do something fresh and new. I hoped it would bring some excitement back into my job.

After some basic training, we grabbed our clipboards and radios and went out with the SWAT team for an evening exercise. We wanted to see how well we could integrate with them. By the time we'd worked together for a couple of hours, the team commander was sold on the concept and the two of us as "tactical dispatchers" officially became members of the SWAT team as a communications unit.

We continued to train together and went out on a call. It was a barricaded subject after a domestic disturbance. That first real SWAT call was nerve-wracking. We hardly knew what we were doing, but we got through it. We did confirm that our skills as dispatchers were valuable to the team at these types of critical incidents.

With that call under our belts, we were determined to train more with the team and see where this new communications system could take us. Sometimes in training, my dispatch partner and I would role-play as the "bad guys" for the team, and on a number of occasions we'd end up bruised and battered. We learned to shoot some weapons that the team members carried and we also learned about their tactics and methods. As we spent more time with the team, they learned to trust us and we learned how to support them. It was a very rewarding experience as we built relationships and learned to depend upon each other as teammates and "brothers." The camaraderie and the challenge of this special assignment were both important factors in reigniting passion for my work. I found myself drawn back to my love for emergency services and I was determined to improve my skills as a dispatcher — both in the field and in the dispatch center.

*****

Early in 2005, after my shift, my boss pulled me aside and shared that he was planning to retire later in the year. I knew he wanted me to apply for his position. I had discussed the possibility with him before and knew he'd worked to prepare me for the day the position would be available. I had been training new dispatchers for several years and had been doing most of the scheduling. He had also taught me how to assist him in preparing the annual budget. While I knew he expected me to apply for the job, I wasn't sure I was right for it. Since Anna's death, I had questioned my abilities and wasn't sure I wanted the responsibility of overseeing an operation that I knew firsthand was often linked to death.

One of my good friends at dispatch encouraged me to pursue the position. She was convinced I was the right person for the job and was sure it would be offered to me if I applied for it. I wasn't so confident in that and still wasn't sure I wanted it, but I decided I would try. My dispatch partner and friend on the SWAT team was also interested in the director position, so my boss arranged for each of us to cover for him when he took some time off. My partner was to cover the first two-week stretch and I would cover the last two weeks.

A few days before my opportunity to act as director, we received a late-night page that the SWAT team was being deployed to another barricaded subject call. We rushed to meet up for the mission, and once on the scene, started preparing the command post a couple of blocks down the street from where the suspect was. This was only our second call, but we understood our role on the team and were excited to put into practice what we had learned in training.

The situation seemed to be moving toward a peaceful resolution, as negotiators had been speaking with the suspect by telephone so it surprised us when we heard gunshots. It was hard to tell how many. I remember thinking it was unfortunate that the suspect hadn't cooperated and that the team was forced to shoot him, but I was shocked when I heard over the radio that it wasn't the suspect who was hit. Two of our teammates had been shot.

The command post immediately became very busy as we requested resources and made phone calls. I called the local hospital and pleaded with them to make sure they would have enough staff available to treat the two officers. When she asked what their condition was, all I could say was they had gunshot wounds. I had no idea how bad off they were.

We didn't know who was shot, so I started paying close attention to whose voices I heard on the radio. It didn't take long to realize which of my teammates weren't talking. For quite a while, as we continued working, we didn't know the extent of their injuries, but there was a point when we thought we heard the commander say that the injuries were *not* life-threatening. I don't know if we heard him wrong or if he didn't have accurate information when he spoke, but we were later informed that one of the men had multiple injuries and the other teammate had died.

We all left the scene sort of shell-shocked. It was hard to believe that call had led to tragedy. It was strange that our team member, and friend, was gone. We thought the situation would resolve peacefully and couldn't believe the turn of events. It was unnerving to realize that something like that could happen in a small town in Kansas. We mourned as a team, as a dispatch center, as an emergency services family and as a community.

My first day as interim director of 911 was also the day of the funeral. I tried to meet the emotional needs of the dispatchers I was responsible for, but I really didn't know how to do that. There were funeral details that involved the dispatch center that I had to organize as well. A group of us from dispatch went to the funeral — I was very moved by the service. The officer was well known and well liked in the community, and I was glad we could go and pay our respects.

On the way to the cemetery, my van, which was full of dispatchers, marveled at the crowds of people that lined the streets. When we passed by a school, we saw the students lined up holding signs expressing their sorrow over our fallen friend. Seeing the children brought a lot of emotion to those of us in the van. Nobody spoke. The only sounds that could be heard were choked-back sobs.

At the end of the burial service, the sheriff called dispatch on the radio and requested a final page for our friend. As my partner and I joined the SWAT team for the last dispatch, I listened to the solemn words spoken by the veteran dispatcher: "He will be missed."

When I arrived home that evening, I was still very sad. Several times during the days following this man's death, I was taken back to the loss of Anna, who had died only a few months earlier. I had experienced a lot of tragedy and pain in a short amount of time and I wasn't coping well with any of it, but, for some reason, I felt like I was where I was supposed to be. It was that day that I finally knew dispatch was my calling and I felt passionate about pursuing the position for the director of communications.

CHAPTER 15

As life would have it, the passing of time affected my sorrow. It moved a little further away every day and I didn't miss it. When Anna had been gone for about nine months, I made the decision to begin writing our story. While I was still very lonely for her and was still grieving, I was also beginning to gain victory over my sorrow and felt God wanted me to share that hope with others. I had never written a book, so there was an element of mystery to it and I wasn't entirely sure I was capable of completing such a big job. I'd always enjoyed writing letters to my friends, but I knew it'd be entirely different organizing and typing hundreds of pages versus writing a page or two. Besides, I wasn't sure when I'd have time to write it. After all, I was a busy momma to five children. I was a home-schooling mom, too, which meant I was never completely alone. I decided the only time I would be able focus on the project was in the quiet of the night, after everybody was in bed. Between the hours of 10:00 pm and 2:00 am became my writing time. In order to be able to follow that schedule, I forced myself to lie down with the little boys every day for a nap. I'm surprised I had enough brain power left at night to write, but the fact that it did work was proof to me that God was in it. Somehow I burned the midnight oil over and over again and it never ran out.

I'd kept a journal off and on for many years, and I turned to it while I was writing. It wasn't organized and included a lot of ramblings, schedules, recipes and other things that wouldn't help me with my book, but I enjoyed the reminiscing. I also thought it was ridiculous how many schedules I didn't keep, and how many times I wrote in my journal about feeling "frazzled." My life as a momma to little children had certainly been hectic.

I knew it was God's prompting to write the book. I couldn't be certain about God's purpose, but I did know that I wanted future generations of the Kraft family to have it as a testimony of God's grace and power. I think I secretly hoped that somewhere along the way it would minister to other hurting parents and even inspire those who hadn't lost children. I wanted others to witness the God who comforted me in my grief and gave me hope on hopeless days. I knew if I could sincerely testify of his presence in my life, that it would create excitement in the lives of those who would read it.

I decided to start my book in 1988 — the year we got married. I didn't write about it then, but I was taken back to our first months of marriage. They were fiery and passionate. I remember a particular argument Kyle and I had. We were in his little Subaru, probably on our way to a fast-food restaurant, when we began to argue. The intensity quickly grew and suddenly, without warning, Kyle pulled into a Quik Trip parking lot in the middle of Wichita, threw off his seatbelt (almost breaking the window in the process), shoved the door open, got out and began to walk. I didn't know where he was going, and in fact wasn't quite sure where I was. I moved to the driver's seat and began following him. He refused to get back in the car, but eventually, feeling conspicuous with all the people watching, I surrendered and said, "C'mon, Honey, pleeeeeez get back in the car. I'm sorry." My apology got him back in the car and I proceeded to drive us home — in silence.

We were so immature and had such materialistic goals. All we knew of life was good jobs, nice houses, cool cars and fancy restaurants, but at that time we were only dreaming of those things. In reality we had low-paying jobs, a small rented house in a poor neighborhood, cheap cars that broke down all the time and Hamburger Helper for supper. When we did eat out (which was actually way too much), we ate hot links with sauerkraut and mustard at Pickles Café or at the infamous Taco Bell. If it was payday, we'd sometimes splurge and go to Pizza Hut for our favorite, thin crust, beef and mushroom pizza. Remembering back to those days was fun ... and eye opening. Our lives looked completely different now.

I was also reminded of the strange circumstances regarding

the revealing of my first pregnancy. I had been sick with a bad cold and had gone to the doctor. He wanted to take an x-ray of my chest to see if I had pneumonia, but wanted to make sure I wasn't pregnant before doing so. I hadn't thought about it at all and didn't think I was, but to be safe I said, "No, I don't think I am."

Because I couldn't say for certain, he said, "Well, let's check first, just to make sure." I was fine with that, and didn't expect to be pregnant. I was shocked when the doctor pulled me into the room and said, "The bad news is, we can't take an x-ray, but the good news is, it's because you're pregnant!"

I looked at him completely shocked and said, "Really? Whoa." I think I forgot I was sick and just floated out of that office not entirely aware of what was going on around me. Being pregnant brought new and interesting emotions that began to change me.

As I wrote, I thought about all the children I'd had since then and yet I still remembered what that first pregnancy felt like.

Nobody would have ever called me "motherly." I never gave children much thought. I didn't even consider having a ring bearer or flower girl in our wedding. I didn't really know any little children anyway, so I'm not sure I even had that option. I looked at children in overalls and thought they looked stupid. I saw snot coming out of their noses and felt like throwing up. Yes, "un-motherly" would describe me perfectly. I babysat one or two times during my teen years and I'm surprised the children survived! I had never changed a diaper. I knew nothing of bottles or how to warm them. I cringe now when I remember allowing a five-year-old girl I was babysitting to walk down the street, by herself, to a neighbor's house! When she asked me if she could go, I ignorantly said, "okay," not giving it a second thought!

Being pregnant with my firstborn, though, instantly changed my attitude toward children. I began to notice them everywhere and suddenly thought they were the most precious creatures walking the earth, especially in their overalls!

When Jared was a year old, I got pregnant with our second child, Samuel. It was emotionally challenging as I reflected on and wrote about that pregnancy, and about the day that we were told our second-born son would die. I hadn't been used to trials in my life, and that one was a doozey. I wasn't accustomed to seeing my husband cry, not the way he cried the day we found out our son would die. We could have pulled away from each other in our grief like so many married couples do, but, thankfully, God drew us close to one another and we clung tightly.

We were new Christians and I'm very grateful that we found Christ before we faced that heartache. We shared that trial because that was *our* baby. We were in it together. God used both of us to create Samuel, and we both loved him simply because he was ours. It didn't matter what he would become or who he would be. It simply mattered that he was our baby — a little piece of each of us. We suffered knowing he wouldn't grow up by our side ... that we'd never really get to know him while on this earth, and we were never the same after his death. He changed the way we lived and the way we viewed life. God used our baby boy, who was born with no brain, to change us forever.

My book would tell stories about failed business ventures, strained friendships, spiritual growth, personal challenges, fun times, sad times, pride and insecurities. I reminisced about the healthy births, the home birth and the births that caused tears. I cried over my pains and rejoiced in my victories.

Writing became especially challenging when I began to share about the morning Anna died. I knew I needed to tell the whole story in detail. Kyle was the one on the phone with 911, but I tried to remember what I heard him saying. I never asked him if it was a man or woman he was talking to. I never thought about a real person being on the other end. I knew when I wrote about that morning, I wasn't getting every detail right, but I could only write the way I remembered it. If the details were wrong, it was at least my memory of it at the time.

That morning was foggy to say the least. I lived it, but in complete shock, barely aware of any of it. I went through the actions of CPR, not knowing if I was doing it right and never questioning. I just followed Kyle's lead and breathed into Anna when he told me to.

I relived each moment of that morning in detail. I heard Anna scream from her bed and the fear came back to me. I moved on to the bathroom and relived the moments while we talked as she took a bath. I thought about the anxiety I had and the pain she had. I was reminded of the next morning — the morning after she died — our first morning without her. The shock had worn off and the reality of Anna really being gone had settled in. She wasn't coming back, and I felt it to the depths of my soul that morning. It hurt like nothing ever had. As I wrote, I grieved all over again.

Kyle always slept next to me while I wrote. Sometimes he'd wake up to my pecking at the laptop keyboard. He'd look at me, touch my arm and say something, then go back to sleep. It was his way of saying, "I'm proud of you." I appreciated the way he supported me, and my project. Sometimes, before he'd go to sleep, he would let me read portions of my writing to him and he'd give me feedback. Occasionally, he wouldn't agree with something and I'd have to decide whether I'd leave it or change it. I usually agreed with what he recommended.

One day — in the wee hours of the morning — I began to sob while writing about Anna's death. I felt the grief so strongly that I couldn't hold back. I wanted Kyle to wake up, but it must have been a long, hard day because he didn't even stir. I could have woken him, but I have such a hard time admitting I have emotional needs. I can't seem to get myself to ask for help very easily. Instead of waking him on purpose, I just cried louder in hopes that he'd hear me, but he didn't. When I was all cried out, I decided to go a different route in asking for help. I'd ask for prayer by sending an email out to some of my family and friends. I explained in the email how terribly painful it was to write about the morning Anna died and I asked them to hold me up in prayer. I hit "send" at about 1:00 am.

*****

We met the Brummett family a few months after Anna died. They had three little girls. Victoria was their oldest and very close to Anna's age. She had dark hair and dark eyes, and reminded me of Anna. They had moved into our cottage (a small house on our property behind our main house) while they were waiting to make a move to Texas after Derrick secured a job there.

Derrick came over the day after I sent the email about needing prayer. He was anxious to tell me something. He said he had gone to bed the previous night at his usual time. Then he teared up as he said, "I had a dream that Victoria died last night." I let my face express my sadness for him because I personally knew just how real dreams could be. I stood there patiently while he composed himself.

"I couldn't get back to sleep, so I decided to get up and check my email," he went on. Just after 1:00 am, he saw the email I had sent begging for prayer. He said, "I stopped right then and prayed for you."

Derrick knew it had been a divine calling and said, "It was only a dream, but it devastated me. I can't imagine what it would be like to really live that. When I woke up I was grateful it wasn't reality, but it *is* your reality."

I was moved and comforted. I rejoiced over that because, once again, I was witnessing God at work. I was sorry that Derrick had to have that dream, but I was grateful he saw it for what it was. God had given him an opportunity to bear my burden, if only through a dream and a prayer. And God was showing me that I could trust Him. My husband didn't need to wake up to comfort me that night. He was resting peacefully. God gave Derrick a heart of sadness to understand what I must have been going through, plus gave him a heart of compassion that prompted him to pray. Derrick prayed for me in my hour of need, when I was too weak to pray for myself.

CHAPTER 16

It was the day the board was going to be interviewing for the communications director position. I had been nervous ever since I put in my application. I was fairly confident with my resume and knew my experience would increase my chances of getting the job, but I was still nervous. My interview was scheduled for right after lunch and I hoped that satisfied stomachs would play in my favor!

I had been preparing for my interview for several weeks. I even bought a suit — the first one I ever owned. I rarely got dressed up for anything and I wasn't very good at putting on a tie. After fighting with it for a while, I just had to let it be and hope it worked well enough.

I had been studying radio and telephone systems so I could speak intelligently about 911 Center technology. My hope was to know more about the technology than the interviewers did. I hoped nothing they asked would go over my head.

Before my interview, I had another appointment that I was also nervous about. I had a subpoena to appear at district court that morning in regards to a police case I had been involved in. I wasn't required to testify in court very often, but it did happen occasionally. I found it intimidating to get up on the stand and answer questions about my actions.

I was still working the night shift at that time, so after I got off work I had to go home and stay awake for a couple of hours before going to court, and then on to my interview. I knew it was going to be a very long day.

When I arrived at the courthouse, I was told I wasn't needed to testify after all. Instead, I met with the deputy who had the case and talked to the attorneys involved. After leaving, I stood outside with the deputy for a few more minutes. We were friends and SWAT teammates. I told him about my interview and we talked about the position for a while. When it was time for me to head off, he wished me luck and said, "You should probably zip your pants up before your interview." If I'd had any confidence at all, it left me at that moment! I had handled official business and then chatted with the deputy outside with my fly open the whole time! I guess I had concentrated too much on my tie.

I knew what it was like to be interviewed before a board. I'd done that when I first applied for the 911 dispatcher position. I remembered how stressful it had been to be up in front of many people, being scrutinized through a barrage of questions. I was dreading having this interview done in the same format. I knew it would be long and taxing.

The panel would include people from the Police and Fire

departments. There would be city officials, the county emergency manager, county commissioners and the county administrator. Ten or 12 people on the panel would conduct the interview process and give their recommendation on hiring. Ultimately, it would be up to the county commission to make the official appointment.

When I arrived, I was directed to a chair. Because of the layout of the room, people were on every side of me … I was center stage. I recognized everybody there but hadn't actually met most of the people. I knew they were well above me in status and pay, and I felt very small as I sat there. Once we got started and I settled into answering the questions, my nerves also settled and I became comfortable with the interview. I was thankful nothing caught me off guard. I confessed to the board that I wasn't a technology expert, but that I felt I had sufficient knowledge to oversee the 911 systems that were in place.

The interviewers seemed satisfied with most of my answers and by the end of the questioning everybody was fairly relaxed, including me. I left feeling satisfied that it had gone well and I was surprised to realize I'd actually enjoyed it. My only concern was that I knew the other applicant had much more experience and knowledge than I did, so I wasn't sure I would be selected.

When I got home that afternoon, I called Jo to tell her it was over and ended with the words, "We'll just have to wait and see." I went to bed to try and rest a little bit before

I had to go back to work for the night, but I couldn't sleep. I was exhausted but overstimulated by the events of the day. Sometime later in the afternoon I was finally able to drift off into a light sleep.

I hadn't been resting long when I heard the phone ring. My caller ID revealed it was a call from the county courthouse. I picked up the phone and was speaking to the county administrator. He informed me that the county commission wanted to offer me the position of director of communications. He asked if I'd like to accept the position and of course I immediately said, "Yes, yes I would."

*****

There was a rapid transition from dispatcher to manager and I was given the opportunity to train for several weeks with my boss before he retired. All I knew well was dispatch, so training proved to be very important. I didn't realize all that went on behind the scenes. We packed in as much as we could in those weeks. Not only was I inheriting a job with many responsibilities, but also big projects that were still in the early stages.

I was also given the opportunity to hire an assistant director, a new position for our department. My outgoing boss had convinced the county that an assistant was needed, and with the transition it was a perfect time to bring one in. So, on top of everything else, I had to figure out who I would appoint as my assistant.

My tactical dispatch partner was the person I chose. Together, we set out to manage the 911 Center. We didn't understand everything, but we had big dreams about where we wanted to take the operation.

My management philosophy supported a productive, fun, low-stress environment. I wanted my team to enjoy working for me. I wanted to be their friend and manage them carefully and honestly. I believed in treating them with the utmost respect at all times. I also hoped to create policies that would minimize the stress they felt from management. I believed this type of leadership would free them to focus on providing quality service, and I knew they'd be happier in their jobs.

For the first couple of months that summer, it appeared my management philosophy was working well. Morale among the dispatchers was high and we were having a good time working together. As I became neck-deep in a radio tower project, I found my time so consumed in understanding the details of it that I wasn't able to focus on the dispatchers or the day-to-day operations like I wanted to. I hoped I'd be able to make up for lost time when I got a handle on the project.

It took me a while to get into the groove. There were new challenges every day. I didn't always move forward in my new responsibilities, but I was learning to understand things better and was optimistic that everything would come together.

*****

While putting in so many hours at work, I wasn't spending much time at home. Jo understood where my priorities had to be at the time, but I think it saddened her that I missed so many family things that summer. Most days I didn't see her much, but she would often share stories with me about what the kids were doing. I knew I was missing out, but I didn't know what else to do. I was so busy and there was just too much to keep up with.

Taylor was eight years old and was taking swimming lessons. I never did get the chance to see him swim, but it was fun to hear about how much he enjoyed it. He also started jumping off the high dive — a big feat for an eight-year-old boy! He had reason to be proud. Jo loved taking Taylor to the pool each day and talking to the other moms there.

Hannah was now four and also went for a swim, but not in the city pool. She took one in our backyard pond by the deck, which was filled with caterpillar-covered lily pads. Hannah loved those caterpillars and thought it would be neat to catch one to give to her big brother. She leaned over the edge of the rocks to reach for one and went down, head-first, right into the water! Jo decided right then and there that Hannah would take swimming lessons the following summer.

Since Jo and I were both working and I was especially consumed in my work, we had little time alone. We were seldom able to go out together. Jo was always patient and demanded nothing from me. She had adapted to our routine and, unfortunately, we simply co-existed. It wasn't that we weren't close or happy, we just didn't prioritize our relationship. She did her thing and I did mine. We both shared in taking care of the kids, but we always worked opposite schedules so there weren't many times that we were all together as a family either.

This lack of unity was not usually much of an issue to me. I was content to be on my own in the evenings with the kids. When Jo came home from work late at night, she'd find me on the computer, listening to music, playing games or watching a movie. We would say hello and goodnight and just kind of pass by each other. I don't suppose we had the type of marriage that she had imagined we would when we were dating, but it seemed to work for us. Even though our work kept us very busy and our family was often apart, somehow we functioned well enough. I think we were both hopeful that there was light at the end of the tunnel ... somewhere in the distance.

CHAPTER 17

When my grief wasn't so overwhelming and life began to demand moving forward, I became very bothered that Anna was buried so far away from home. It was as if we left her in a foreign land. Not only was I lonely for her, but I felt as though she was lonely for me too. While logic and common sense should have told me differently, they didn't ... I needed her near me.

It never bothered me that Samuel and Josiah were buried in Derby. We lived in and near Derby when they died, but it had never been Anna's home — she'd lived in Sedgwick her whole life. We'd never planned where we would bury Anna if she died. We'd never talked about a funeral. We just assumed she would grow up and have children and grand-children. It would have been impossible to survive thinking any differently.

I'm glad we never took time to think about such things, but now I envisioned Anna being frightened and feeling abandoned, and I felt guilty because I hadn't thought through things better. Her death took us by surprise. We didn't know what steps to take in planning her ending. We decided things carelessly. We simply didn't have the energy to do it any other way. The day we buried her I knew she was in the wrong place, but it was too late to change my mind. The cloud of grief grew thicker and I felt more desperate. I was lost in that cloud.

We didn't visit Anna's grave for several months. In fact, the day we did visit the cemetery was quite by accident. It was May 21, 2005. We had just had lunch in Derby at Pizza Johns with my family and some friends who were visiting from Arizona. When we were walking out the door, my dad suggested, "Hey, you could stop by the cemetery." He didn't know that we'd avoided going … that I feared going. What kind of mommy was I? I didn't want him to think I didn't care (although he would never think that), because that was exactly the opposite of how I felt. I cared too much.

When we drove into the cemetery, we couldn't remember where Anna was buried. We didn't see her marker the first time through, so we drove through again, very slowly. Finally, I spotted it. There was Anna's little metal marker right before my eyes. I said, "Honey, stop. There it is." I hated that we hadn't been able to afford a stone for her. I think that's one of the reasons I didn't want to go to the cemetery. I cringed when I saw her grave marked only by an imprinted piece of ugly metal. We'd spent so much money on her funeral and every other thing related to her death (including our consoling indulgences), and because of that we hadn't yet been able to afford the stone she deserved. The tiny little marker simply read:

Anna Gabrielle Kraft
7/25/98 - 11/19/04

Deep emotion engulfed me and I wished we'd stayed away. Nobody would get out of the car at first, but then Kyle and I did. Only Silas would get out with us. We walked up to the grave and just stood there with our backs to the van. Silas began to run around, completely unaware of the depth of our pain. We didn't make him stop playing. He was only three years old, he didn't know. My heart broke and my body froze as I pictured Anna's precious little body lying there six feet underground. We stood there completely quiet and still. Tears filled my eyes and began to drip off my nose. I didn't put my hands to my face to wipe them away because I didn't want the kids in the van to see me crying. When Kyle put both of his arms around me, I let my head rest on his chest and then I heard Cecily begin to cry. She'd never been one to hold in emotion and she didn't then either. It was desperate and inconsolable. I ceased crying for my loss and began crying for hers. I only felt Cecily's pain. I wanted Anna to be here for her. It seemed so unfair that Cecily had to be without her closest friend. She was only eight years old and was being called to endure such horrible heartache. Now she was the very middle child of five — she must have felt so alone without Anna.

I stood there and imagined Christ coming for us at that moment. I pictured us all going to Heaven together — including Anna and the boys who were buried just a few yards away. I didn't want to endure the pain and I didn't want my kids to hurt any longer. I was sick of grief. I was worn out and tired of hurting.

Initially, the drive home was bad. Nobody talked. The sorrow had penetrated deeply and nobody dared say anything until our emotions were under control. If I had been alone, I would have screamed. I would have pounded my fists. I would have cried out loud until nothing else came. But my children needed me to be strong for them.

At some point, I mustered up the courage to say, "I'm so glad I still have all of you. You're so special to me." Then we all talked about how blessed we were to have a close family. The remainder of the drive was peaceful and productive as we reflected on our love and our hope in eternity … together.

After our visit to the cemetery, I confessed to Kyle that I hated that Anna was buried in Derby. I had cried to him about it many times, but I never did ask him to move her. I knew it would be expensive and I also knew we couldn't move Anna without also moving Samuel and Josiah. I just knew I would feel I was betraying my baby boys if I took their sister from them. I loved Samuel and Josiah so much, and even though I had less time getting to know them, they were still mine and I loved them. Kyle understood my sorrow and told me we'd try to move Anna and the boys when we had some money. I believed him, but feared that day would never come.

*****

One Year Later ...

Kyle bought some plots in the Sedgwick cemetery down the road from our house. He planned everything. The only thing he asked for my help with was choosing the location in the cemetery to bury our children. There was a fresh, new section without graves and it was assumed that I would want a spot in that area. It was so clean and nice, but I didn't want to bury our children there because it seemed so lonely. I didn't want my kids to be by themselves. It was a strange way to think, I knew that, but it's where my mind went.

Kyle took our son Jared, who was 15 at the time, to the Sedgwick cemetery to begin digging the holes for Samuel and Josiah's caskets. A man had been hired to dig Anna's larger hole with a backhoe. Kyle was to bring our children home the following day. On an overcast day in May, Kyle drove to Derby to dig up the graves. He left the rest of us at home, knowing it would be too difficult for us. When he got to the cemetery, men were there to volunteer their help. Kyle didn't know most of them, but through a series of events and conversations, men showed up to ease Kyle's burden and I was so grateful.

Later, Kyle told me that after the graves were opened, a big flatbed truck with an arm picked up Anna's larger vault and placed it on the truck's bed. Kyle carefully lifting Samuel's and Josiah's tiny caskets out one at a time, carried them over to the truck and placed them next to Anna's. He then followed the truck on the 45-minute drive to the Sedgwick cemetery. I can only imagine how difficult that was for him. I will forever love him more for that sacrifice he made for me.

It was drizzling rain when Kyle called me from his cell phone to tell me they were on their way. About the time I knew they'd arrive, the rain began to pour down. I sat at home, watched the rain and worried about Kyle and the heart-wrenching task that was in front of him. I felt guilty for asking him to do it, but was too afraid to go and be with him. I was grateful he hadn't required anything of me, but as I sat there with *What About Bob* on the television, I felt guilty too. It didn't seem fair to let him go through that alone.

My love for Kyle won out over my fear, and I knew I needed to go and make sure he was okay. Abigail, who was almost 13 at the time, wanted to go with me. We left Jared and his friend Timothy with the other kids and drove to the cemetery. The flatbed truck was pulling in just as we drove up, Kyle right behind him in his car. We pulled off to the side of the road and watched them get out and begin the process. Seeing the caskets on the flatbed overwhelmed me and I drove away. I thought about going home, but couldn't get myself to do it. I drove around the block, then pulled back up in the same spot on the road. By this time, it was raining very hard and I noticed Kyle digging in the downpour. I saw the truck back up to the graves. I'm not sure what I expected to feel, but immense sorrow flooded my heart.

Kyle saw me but didn't stop working. He had determination written all over his face. When he was done digging, I tearfully watched as he carried the tiny caskets of our baby boys, one at a time, and gently set them down in their appropriate places. I hadn't seen those caskets for many years and all of that grief swept over me once again. I'd had such a short time with Samuel and Josiah and the emotions had numbed considerably through the years. Now I wished I could hold those precious bodies in my arms again.

My heart ached more as the machine hoisted Anna's much larger casket and set it in the larger hole. When it didn't fit, the man lifted it back out, put it on the flatbed, and he and Kyle began digging again. It seemed to take forever. When they had finally dug enough dirt out for Anna's casket to fit, the big claw picked it back up and awkwardly set it down in the hole. I know the man couldn't completely control the movement of the arm, but as it kind of swayed and jerked back and forth, I had to turn my head. The movements were too rough and I wanted him to be gentle with her.

I didn't want to, but I pictured Anna's sweet body in that casket. The same little body that I snuggled and loved was wasting away in that box. I couldn't stand the thought of it. I looked over at Abigail, but no words came. I saw her tears and wished I could spare her the pain, but I couldn't get myself to drive away. My heart swelled with love for my husband. His strength impressed me, but his sacrifice overwhelmed me. There he was in the pouring rain, digging the graves and carrying the caskets of our children, all because of his love for me.

A few days after the caskets were placed, the stones were all put in their places. Samuel's and Josiah's had been removed and stored, and Anna's had been purchased. They were all put together on one piece of cement foundation next to each other, right where they should be.

If I take a particular route to town, I can see those three stones right next to each other as I drive by — the three stones at the heads of the three children that lived in my womb and died in my arms. I don't stop often, but just knowing my children are laid to rest near me matters. When I do drive by their graves, I'm reminded of that day that my husband sacrificed his heart for mine. It was the day he lovingly brought our children home.

CHAPTER 18

I was on call 24-7. My assistant covered every other weekend, but I still needed to be available for any situation that might come up. When my pager went off — for what seemed like the millionth time — I realized I was beginning to hate the constant beeping. Not only did my blood pressure shoot up when it sounded, but my face flushed and I could feel the physiological changes that Pavlovian conditioning brought forth from the completely annoying noise.

I thought, *What is it this time?* A radio channel not working? Another computer crashed? Perhaps one of the dispatchers was mad at another and needed me to mediate their battle of strong self-centered wills. On the other hand, it could be a fire chief or a police officer upset about how we handled a call. I was responsible for every decision that each dispatcher made. Everything had to be done just right. If something went wrong, the fingers always pointed in my direction.

Already feeling angry, I grabbed my pager and saw it was my least favorite issue to handle: a night shift dispatcher calling in sick. My immediate thought was, *Great!* After calling to check in on dispatch, it was obvious nobody was anxious to stay another four hours to help cover the empty shift. Even if they had been willing, how was I going to get somebody to come in at 4:00 am to cover the last half of the shift? So, "I'll be there" is what I found myself saying. I shut off the cordless phone and threw it across the room.

Jo was visibly irritated when I told her I was going to sleep for a couple of hours and then would be going back to work. Her response was, "Again?"

She didn't know how upset I already was with the situation. She was just concerned about me and for our family, but I took it personally and snapped back with, "I don't have a choice in the matter, Jo! I don't want to go in but who else is going to do it?"

I hated when I lost my temper and always felt so guilty. Jo was always so patient with me and didn't deserve my lashing out at her. After lying down, I couldn't sleep. I was so mad at myself for being rude to the dispatcher on the phone, for lashing out at Jo and for letting the kids hear me yell. I knew it scared them when I did that, and I wanted to apologize, but I couldn't get myself to do it.

In just nine months, I had watched my dreams for the dispatch center crumble. I had such high hopes that I would exceed everybody's expectations and that the dispatchers would love coming to work every day. I hoped to be the boss everyone wishes they had, but in actuality I was making things miserable for them. Each step of every project just became another headache, and I couldn't seem to figure things out.

I was working so many hours and living on so little sleep that I didn't have the mental energy to fix the things I had screwed up. I was irritable and often harsh. I could tell that the dispatchers were losing faith in me. When something needed to be brought to my attention, they came to me with hesitation because every problem angered and frustrated me. Morale was low around the center and I perceived there was a lot of bickering and back-stabbing going on. I caught wind of things that were being said about me, and while I knew I deserved it, it also hurt. I was trying so hard and I did care about the dispatch team. I wanted so badly to earn their respect, but I was overwhelmed and failing.

Our 911 Center serves nine different law enforcement agencies, seven different fire departments and five different EMS agencies. Our area of responsibility is roughly 700 square miles with 35,000 citizens. We handle approximately one-hundred twenty 911 calls a day, along with countless other tasks. Unfortunately, we operate on a shoestring staffing level, making it harder to manage than I initially realized.

There were so many agencies to be accountable to and so much technology to stay on top of, that I just wasn't able to spend the time needed on the day-to-day operations. The most important things to focus on were training and quality assurance, and those were the very areas I was neglecting.

Those were the programs I vowed to improve when I was promoted, but in my effort to be a good director and stay on top of everything else, I just couldn't seem to get to them. Those failures were what caused the dispatchers to lose faith in me. Those failures were ultimately what made them unhappy with their jobs.

*****

When I became director, I was moved to the day shift. That was the only time I could handle much of the business I needed to take care of. When Jo switched to the day shift, it was the first time in our marriage that we were working the same shift and were actually together in the evenings. We expected this change to work well and were excited about it. We were also looking forward to being together more as a family. We thought it would be a better situation for all of us, but because frustration, depression and anger dominated my life, I didn't contribute much to the family. I spent many hours at home brooding over the sad state of my life. I dwelt on the negative and continually complained about having to do so many things I hated. I was often so low on energy that I just left Jo to manage the house and spend time with the kids. I usually found something to do alone that would drown out my thoughts. I was worthless company.

When a specific problem arose that I didn't have a solution to, I became fearful and constantly worried. I convinced myself that worrying was productive because I was processing the problem in my head. In actuality, I was just becoming anxious and obsessed with the unresolved issues. The worry and fear didn't lead to solutions; they led to pain. I did all the same things I always did to try to numb that pain. I buried myself in music, books, movies and games. Once again, it was my way of withdrawing from the world. I isolated myself from everybody, including my family. I attempted to escape my life.

Some days were happier, when my emotions weren't so raw and I was more involved at home with my family. I loved having good days, when I could function as a loving daddy and husband. I found such fulfillment in mustering up the energy and courage to be that man. I enjoyed playing with my kids. I just wished every day could be like that.

Jo and the kids learned how to read me. From the moment I walked in the door, they began analyzing my mood. It was then that they'd either make an effort to engage in activity and conversation with me or go off to do something else. In my emotional instability, Jo and the kids couldn't even count on me when it seemed everything was okay. I took offense to things so easily that even a wrong look set me off. Sometimes even an innocent comment would offend me. While I could always feel the emotions coming on, I had no control over them. They consumed and controlled me. As much as I hated it, I felt powerless to change.

CHAPTER 19

The book wasn't a quick project, but it didn't take nearly as long as I thought it would. It was May 2006, about nine months after I started, that I found myself wrapping it up. While I felt a great deal of satisfaction over completing an entire book, I also felt very insecure about it. I didn't lack confidence in the story itself, but in the way I told it. Was it sufficient? Was I only pretending to be a writer? Only time would tell.

I sent my manuscript to a service called The Writer's Edge, and for a fee they evaluated and rated my manuscript. I was so excited when I got good results from their evaluation! They approved my book to be added to a list that would be sent to publishers and agents. I had an ignorant view of the publishing world. I was just sure in no time I'd be a published author.

I contacted every single publisher and agent that I found while searching the Internet. I also bought *Sally Stuart's Christian Market Writer's Guide* and contacted more people that I saw listed in her book. I didn't hear back from most of them, but the ones I did hear back from sent simple form letters with my name in the greeting telling me something like, *No thank you, but don't give up!*

One publisher actually called me and barely spoke English. I had to repeat, "Excuse me?" so many times, it was embarrassing. I found myself praying frantically, "Lord, please help me to understand this man." Listening very carefully, I was able to understand that he wanted to publish my book, but under one condition — I would be required to pay for the first 5,000 copies! I thought I was getting somewhere until I realized it would be about $30,000 out of my pocket, which would have been impossible since we barely had $300 in the bank. It was clear that I had a very long road ahead of me.

I had friends and family read my book and was grateful for the feedback. I changed the format of the second half when a friend told me she was "bored" reading it. It wasn't easy hearing her frank words, but that's why I asked her to read it, because I knew that particular friend would be completely open and honest in her critique. I also changed things that I had incorrect details about and corrected some other errors, but my confidence grew as I was told how "inspirational" and "wonderful" my book was.

As I continued to pursue publishing, I broke rules and sent my proposal to people I was told not to. I had an unrealistic notion that somebody would stumble upon it and publish it. I was told very bluntly, "Your stories are a dime a dozen," and "Why would anybody publish your story? You're a nobody." A large Christian organization rejected my proposal and even offered me counseling. I learned that most publishers have protocol for dealing with people like me. They compliment you on your great success at completing a book and then encourage you to continue to pursue publishing. I remember thinking, *Uh huh, and exactly how is that going to happen if I'm turned down by everybody and I don't have any money to pursue self-publishing?*

It was at that point that I gave up, I really did. I lost heart and gumption. I quit. I was done looking for a publisher, an agent or even an interview. I began to think that my new venture as an author would end before it really got started. Every door I tried to open was locked tight. I decided if any of them were going to open, it was going to be because God intervened on my behalf. I would just wait, and while I waited, life would simply move forward. I hoped my efforts weren't in vain as I tried to console myself by thinking, *At least my family will have our story for future generations,* and I guess, in a way, I meant it.

*****

Practically from the day Anna died, I begged God for another daughter. I knew that nothing and no one would ever take the place that Anna held in my heart, and I wasn't looking for a replacement, but I craved the little girl I'd lost and thought somehow having another daughter would help to ease that pain.

God didn't answer those prayers on my timetable; He rarely does. Maybe it's because He knows how desperately I need to learn patience. It wasn't until the end of 2006 that I found out I was expecting. The baby was due July 25, 2007 — Anna's birthday. That confirmed it for me. Not only was God going to give me another daughter, but He was going to give her to me on Anna's birthday!

We had a sonogram in March 2007 and I had to laugh at myself — our next baby was not going to be another daughter, but another son. I grieved in my heart for a moment — not for the boy I would have — no, I already loved him, but for the little girl I still wouldn't have. In reality, I wasn't disappointed at all, I was just still grieving and looking for something to satisfy the longing in my heart for the little girl I was missing.

Harrison Tate graced our world on July 29, 2007. He was our biggest baby at 9 lbs. 5 oz., and was stubborn about making his appearance! I didn't think he'd ever leave his watery world. As soon as I held him, I couldn't imagine life with any other baby. This was the child I was supposed to have.

*****

As a last-ditch effort, I submitted my book manuscript to a publisher in October 2007, and quite to my surprise, on November 19, 2007, the three-year anniversary of Anna's death, I got the call I'd been waiting for. It was from a publisher who was offering to make my story into a book. The fact that they called on *that* day made me see that God's hand was in it. I knew there was significance to that. Of course, I was hoping somebody would pay me to publish my book — not the other way around — but that's not the way it happened, and honestly, at this point, I wasn't the least bit surprised. With this publisher, I would have to invest $4,000. That was a far cry from $30,000 and at least *In Faithfulness, He Afflicted Me* would be in print.

Kyle cashed in his 401K to close the deal. I'm embarrassed to admit that it was all the savings we had. When you've had nine children, open-heart surgeries, funerals and the usual expenses that come with a large family, that's just how it is.

While we went through the process of publishing, we talked about what we wanted to do with the book. Kyle and I wondered if God might use us — put us in a ministry of some sort. In an effort to be prepared for this possible ministry, we decided it might be a good idea to have a copy of the 911 call from the morning Anna died. We were terrified to listen to it and weren't sure we actually would, but feared losing the opportunity to have it. So we decided that Kyle would call Harvey County Dispatch and request a copy.

The day Kyle made the call, he was connected with a man named Courtney Becker. Being a salesman and a people-person, Kyle's always been a good communicator and started right in, explaining who he was and what he wanted. Not many situations make him nervous, but when Courtney began to speak, he said it was a bit awkward. The conversation started slowly and Courtney seemed a bit hesitant. Kyle was surprised when Courtney told him that he was the man who took his call the morning Anna died. That caught Kyle off guard and he didn't know what to say.

As Kyle relayed the story to me, it dawned on us for the first time that we'd never thought about that man on the other end of the phone the morning we called 911. Putting a name to that person I'd never thought about was a little strange. For the first time, it sank in that somebody else was part of Anna's last moments on Earth. For some reason, my heart became very tender for him and I wished I knew more about him and what he thought of our situation. Because it had been more than three years since the call, it surprised me he remembered it. I found myself wishing I could ask him some questions, but that was awkward too. I wasn't sure it would be appropriate. I decided to just put the whole thing out of my mind.

When Kyle went to pick up the tape of the call, Courtney handed him a letter with it and told him that Anna's death had really affected his life. Kyle left the envelope sealed until we were together and had me read it out loud.

Mr. and Mrs. Kraft,

When Kyle called me this morning, I was unprepared for the rush of intense emotion that came to me. At the risk of being too forward, I would like to share a few thoughts with you. Though we don't know each other, ever since November 19, 2004, your family has been in my thoughts and prayers. That early-morning call in November has been with me ever since we hung up.

Through 911, I have been involved in countless tragedies, and I have interacted with people on all levels of duress. Those experiences have taught me how to place such difficulties in a context and perspective that always cause me pain but do not cause me to be incapacitated with grief. That call, however, literally devastated me for weeks after. I remember being tearful and easily overwhelmed. I questioned my work and whether I wanted to continue dispatching. I remember my wife not understanding my depression, and I remember breaking down at the dispatch console while reading Anna's obituary. I cut her obituary out and put it in my wallet. I still get tearful when I relate that experience to other dispatchers.

With time, faith and support from my co-workers, I guess I somewhat came to grips with your tragedy. I have always wished there was more I could have done for her and more that I could have done for your family. My prayers were the best I could offer.

It's not often that we realize how people touch the lives of others. I just want you to know how much the passing of Anna and being with you during that painful time for your family has touched my life. In my wallet I still carry her obituary with the very sweet picture of her as a reminder and a

*commitment to always do the best I can in my career. I
believe that commitment, in turn, helps me to help others who
are facing tragedy. So her life and death continue to impact
the lives of others in need in ways that only God knows.*

*Thank you for reading my thoughts, and may God bless
your family.*

Courtney Becker

I barely made it through that letter. I was so choked up as
I read, that when I was done, I just sat and cried. My throat
was so constricted, I couldn't have said anything if I wanted
to. Three years had gone by and God was giving us yet
another reason to rejoice, another consolation to the pain
we'd suffered. This man's life and career were changed
because of our little girl.

My book was in the process of being published and I knew
I wanted that letter in it. I asked Kyle if he would get Courtney's
permission to add the letter as an afterword in my book.
Courtney said, "Yes." I still had never met him personally,
but felt connected to him and hoped I'd be able to meet him
at some point. I wasn't ready for that quite yet, though.

*****

A few months later ... August 2008

I walked to the mailbox, hoping to find the first copy of
my book. It wasn't official (it was one for me to proofread),

but it was the only book I'd ever written and I was excited. When I pulled the puffy yellow envelope out of the mailbox, I tore it open as quickly as I could. I felt stupid for the dorky, childish grin I had on my face. I just stood there staring at it. This was my book and there was my name, my picture and my title. I turned it over in my hands and began to walk back to the house, feeling very glad I lived in the country (so nobody could see me being so childlike).

The only people at home were the younger children. They were playing outside so I held the book up and yelled, "Look, guys! I'm an official authoress!" They ran towards me, Cecily reminding me a lot of myself when she began to scream, dance and get overly excited. She hugged me carelessly, but beautifully, and the little boys grabbed my legs. They were proud of their momma and I don't think I'd been that excited about anything in a very long time.

I proofed the book and sent it back to the publisher to have corrections made. Eventually, printing was completed and I received my shipment of a case of books. That was a day to remember! The kids kept teasing me with titles like, "Miss Author" and "Famous Mom." I just rolled my eyes and said, "Oh brother!" I really think the little ones thought I was suddenly famous.

Kyle and I wanted to go and give Courtney a book. It had been almost four years since the morning Anna died, and I still hadn't met the man who took Kyle's call — the man who tried to comfort him in his distress and who tried to save our daughter. I could tell just by reading his letter that he was a kind man. I appreciated that he took the time to let us know how our daughter had changed his life, and I was ready to give him a warm, sincere hug and thank him for doing his best to help us in the worst moments of our lives. I was a bit nervous about saying something stupid or getting emotional and not being able to talk at all, but did want to meet him.

When we walked into the Harvey County building, I saw a man standing in the lobby with his wife and two children. I assumed it was Courtney and his family. I don't remember exactly what was said first, but I remember giving him that warm hug. I hugged his wife, too. I handed him my book and told him I'd written a note to him in the front. I said, "There's everything you ever wanted to know about the Kraft family ... and then some." He smiled and said he was looking forward to reading it.

At that point, I had no idea if they knew Jesus. I guess I assumed Courtney did since he mentioned his faith in the letter he wrote to us, but how could I know for sure without knowing him? My book, being full of Jesus, would either be familiar to him or be overwhelming to him, but I hoped it would touch his heart either way.

I loved the Becker family right off the bat. They had such a humble and sincere way about them. They were kind and warm and though they didn't know us, they seemed to really care about us. On the way to meet them, I thought about the shows I'd seen on television where the 911 dispatcher gets to meet the victim he saved. I even had the vision in my mind of the family hugging and thanking him for saving their loved one. But this was different. The 911 call was for our daughter, who didn't survive. Was I supposed to react the same way? Was I supposed to show gratitude or sadness? Should I assume he felt bad for us or that he was happy to be of service? I wasn't sure if he'd be cool and professional or warm and caring. The situation was definitely a bit unusual, but I did what my heart told me to do. I sincerely thanked him for trying to save our daughter.

I asked Courtney what it was that drew him into the call. It was something I'd wondered about ever since receiving his note. He said, "I know now that your daughter's name is Anna, but the morning I took the call I thought Kyle said, 'Hannah,' and that's my daughter's name. Because of that, I personalized Kyle's position and his pain. It gripped my heart."

I looked at Hannah, who was standing between her mom and dad, and felt a bond with her. She was about the same age Anna had been when she died, and while she looked nothing like Anna, she was still a little girl and my heart met with hers for a moment. I knew none of this was by accident.

It had taken me many weeks to forgive myself and realize that Anna's time on Earth was done. God had set a day for her to go and be with Him and no matter what I did, it wouldn't have saved her. I wanted Courtney to know that too. I wanted him to know that we had come to terms with

that and we were at peace. I'm not sure if that conversation
came or not, but I do remember telling him that Anna would
have loved him, and I meant it. She would have.

CHAPTER 20

I usually took a week off at Thanksgiving and a week off at Christmas, and although it made no sense to do that now, I knew I needed to make it happen. I desperately needed time away from work. Jo and I decided to plan a quick getaway to celebrate our anniversary. We never seemed to have the money to take family vacations, so we started a tradition to have a little anniversary getaway every year. Usually we'd take three days and go to a bed and breakfast. It was so nice to be together and escape the stresses of everyday life. The kids enjoyed it, too, because they got to stay with grandparents.

We decided to go to a bed and breakfast near Mulvane, KS, called Aunt Sue's. They had several cottages on a piece of beautiful property, with a duck pond to boot! Each cottage had a private hot tub on the deck. We were able to soak in the tub with the snow falling on us at the same time, a unique and wonderful experience.

It was during these little getaways that Jo and I were able to really just be ourselves. Somehow I was able to put work out of my mind when I knew I wasn't on call. On that anniversary trip, I was able to think clearly for the first time in a long time. We had some refreshing conversations and were able to share pieces of our lives that we hadn't taken the time or had the desire to discuss. It felt great connecting emotionally and bearing each other's burdens without being overwhelmed with our own. It was good to be reminded how much we loved each other. On that trip, we talked about our future, rehashed our dreams and even discussed the possibility of my leaving emergency services someday for a less stressful life.

My time off passed too quickly. Once the holidays were over, the thought of work instantly dampened my spirits. Taylor had the same trouble I did. He was in the fourth grade, and though he was a good student, he didn't enjoy school.

Taylor was a sensitive child, and the chaos of being around a lot of kids seemed to bother him. He wasn't looking forward to going back. I saw a lot of me in him and it concerned me. I worried he might grow up with the same issues I had, and I didn't want that for him.

Hannah, on the other hand, was thrilled to go back to school. She was a first grader and often reminded us that we should stop treating her like a kindergartener. She loved her teacher and wanted to be just like her. During her Christmas break she set up her own little classroom. Her 'students' learned all the wonderful things she taught them, but her students also had their fair share of behavioral issues. These imaginary children were very dysfunctional and her teaching time was quite limited by all of her scolding. It was really cute to watch, but a bit disturbing too. I wondered if some of her role-playing was a reflection of my parenting.

The rut that I had been in before the holidays didn't disappear while I was away. I went right back to dreading each and every day. I had still not adjusted to my role as director and nothing was improving. While I might have been getting better at pretending the problems weren't there, I hadn't improved at all at coping. I was totally overwhelmed and hadn't figured out how to responsibly manage everything and everyone in my department.

I had two big projects for the year, and while they were both necessary, I knew they would each present a lot of challenges to the dispatchers. We had to replace our 911 telephone system and our main computer software system that we used for nearly all of our duties. Because of the repetitive nature of dispatching, the dispatchers had become very familiar with the routine they were required to perform. The tasks had become easy. The new system would create new procedures and I knew it would be very difficult to adapt to something new. Change is not easy in any workplace, but in the communications center I knew it would become a crisis if it wasn't handled well.

I was filled with dread over what I knew was going to be a long and hard year. I also feared losing my job if I didn't proceed very carefully. I'd considered the possibility of failing, and I almost didn't care. Maybe I wasn't cut out to be the director.

*****

One morning in my office, while having a particularly difficult day, I received a phone call. The man on the phone said his name was Kyle. When he began to explain to me why he was calling, I knew who he was. I recognized his voice and fell into a bit of a panic. I thought, "Oh my God, so now's the time." I had always wondered if I was going to be confronted by him or his family. I was prepared to hear an accusation, but wasn't prepared to respond. I just knew the day of reckoning had arrived.

Kyle told me that his wife was writing a book and that they were preparing for ministry. Surprisingly, his voice was kind, and he didn't sound angry at all. He asked if it would be possible to get a copy of the telephone call he had made to 911 the morning his daughter died. I debated for a second whether I should tell him that I was there with him that morning. When the silence grew a little awkward and I knew I must go on, I simply said, "I was the one who took your call." I sat there waiting for the hit. At least it would be over, once and for all.

Instead, it was his turn to say nothing. I must have caught him off-guard too. After more awkward silence, I finally said, "I can have that ready for you to pick up in a couple of hours." He thanked me and we hung up.

I put the phone down and sat still and quiet. The moment I'd dreaded for years ended so peacefully … so uneventfully.

It wasn't even really an emotional call as I'd anticipated. It was as though he'd never once thought about me. I'd never considered that possibility. How could he be upset with me if he'd never thought of me? I perceived Anna's daddy was a kind and gentle man.

As I sat there thinking about Kyle and Anna, I played back pieces of the call in my mind. Once again, I heard Kyle's desperate pleas and Anna's involuntary noises. It had been awhile since I had experienced the deep grief over Anna's death. In meetings since then, I'd often been asked to answer the question, "What is the hardest call you've ever taken?" I always responded with the story of that call — the morning I talked to a father for 14 minutes while his little girl lay there dying. Just as I'd always done when rehashing that call to my fellow workers, I felt that wave of sadness come over me. I walked over and closed my office door. My chest felt heavy as I once again choked back the emotion. I was amazed at how easily it returned. I'd had hopes that it had faded.

I took Anna's obituary out of my wallet to check the date of her death so I could pull the file — November 19, 2004. I found the call in our dispatch records and printed it off. I took the printout to my assistant director and asked him to make a recording of the telephone call. I had never listened to that call again and I wasn't about to do it then.

I felt a tremendous need to communicate with Kyle's family about how sad I was over the loss of their daughter. I wasn't sure why I wanted or needed to tell them, but I did.

That's when I began typing a letter. I was apprehensive about inserting my thoughts and emotions into their lives. They had certainly suffered enough and I didn't want to add to their pain. Although I wasn't sure I would actually give the letter to Kyle when he came, I needed to say what was in my heart, if only for my own comfort.

When completed, I put the note in an envelope, set in on my desk with the 911 recording and I waited.

When Kyle arrived, we introduced ourselves. It was an unbelievable moment for me. This man that I had spent so much time thinking about and grieving for was standing directly in front of me. The truth was immediately evident. Not only did he hold nothing against me, but he seemed to have put the details of the call out of his mind. I don't blame him. I would have too, if I could have, but that call was all I had. It tortured me and seemed to deliberately possess me.

As I conversed with him, I realized that Kyle was easy to talk to. I was very relieved by that because I knew I'd be at a loss for words.

We didn't talk for long, but I felt a bond with him. We were two men who had shared a few horrible moments together from very different perspectives. Kyle didn't know I'd suffered, and I couldn't even begin to fathom his suffering. When I handed him the tape, I also handed him the letter. I told him that his daughter's death had impacted my life and that I explained it better in the letter. He smiled, said "thank you," we shook hands and he left.

I closed my office door, walked back to my desk and sat down. I wasn't sure what had just happened or why, but I was glad I'd had that short meeting with Kyle. I found myself hoping I'd hear back from him because I had a feeling the mystery of not knowing what they thought when they read my letter would distract me from my job. However, I also feared hearing back from him. I could only hope I had made the right decision in writing to their family.

*****

I was in the back room at dispatch discussing a very frustrating computer issue with our support vendor when the telephone rang. The call was for me, but had come in on my assistant's line so he handed me the phone. When I realized it was Kyle, uneasiness set in. I was anxious, but also curious to know what he had to say.

It was such a huge relief when Kyle told me that he and his wife were "touched deeply" by the letter I had written to them. I no longer had to wonder if I had made a mistake in giving it to them. He said that his wife wanted to end her book with it. I couldn't believe it. He then asked if I would permit them to use it. I don't know whether I hesitated or not, but since I didn't know their story, I did wonder how that letter would fit in her book. I told Kyle that it was just fine with me. Again, he had a cheerful, kind voice that made me feel at ease. It was a short call, but a pleasant one. When

I hung up, my heart just leapt for joy, not because my letter was going in her book, but because of the healing words of appreciation from Kyle!

*****

Nine months later ...

All my fears about the year were validated once the projects began. The dispatchers were very frustrated with the new computer system, and all the long hours of work I had put in preparing for the installation did nothing to make the transition any smoother. We had all gone through a day of training with the software vendor and then I had personally re-trained each dispatcher on how to use the system. Some features didn't seem to work like we thought they would, others didn't work at all. I realized there was just no way to fully understand what we were getting into and how it would work until we started using it.

From my office, I repeatedly heard the dispatchers complaining about the system throughout the day. When I walked through the dispatch area, I could see the frustration on their faces. Some were fairly aggressive in expressing their hatred of the system. Each complaint and every negative look was like an arrow shot directly at me. I took all of their frustrations personally. It was always my goal to try to keep the dispatchers happy and content, but they were miserable.

There was a lot of data that still had to be entered into the system to make it work. Some dispatchers had previously helped me with that task before we were actually using the system. Now that their frustration was boiling over, I didn't feel I could ask for their help, so I spent my days and evenings entering that data myself. I also tested the system with different methods to see if I could get it to work better for us.

When I finally went home in the evenings, I was a bundle of nerves. I was so filled with anxiety that I could barely think straight. My thoughts would race and pull me in many different directions, none of which were good. I was paranoid. I imagined the dispatchers working against me to get me fired. These imaginary scenarios ran through my mind all the time. No matter how hard I tried to escape the stress of work and the thoughts that came with it, I couldn't. None of my usual methods worked at all. I stayed up very late into the night stewing over things. After sleeping a very short time, I always woke with a feeling of dread and wished I didn't have to go back to work. My back was against the wall and I had no solutions to the problems I was facing.

I had always struggled to sleep because I had such a hard time quieting my mind enough to doze off, but this was worse than I could remember. I was frantic, and there was no peace. I don't know what Jo and the kids thought of me during this time. It had been going on so long. I suppose their silence was an attempt to keep peace with me. I remember Jo telling me that living like we were wasn't worth it and I agreed with her, but I couldn't think of any solution. If I quit my job, how would I support my family? Jo didn't care about the financial consequences. She just wanted her husband back.

*****

One day in late August, I was in the hospital with my mom. She had suffered a mild stroke but was recovering. She knew I hadn't been doing well, and as we talked, she told me that she was very concerned for me. She asked me a question that kind of surprised me. She asked if I had considered harming myself. In my pride I wanted to laugh and call it nonsense, but I also wanted to answer it honestly. When I was a teen, I did have suicidal thoughts. My parents knew that. I had always been so vulnerable to depression, but after a failed attempt as a teen, I committed to never doing it again. I saw the suffering it caused those who loved me and knew it was not the answer to life's problems. So I could honestly tell her, "No, I hadn't considered harming myself," and it was the truth. I wouldn't ever do it again.

Having been on 911 calls that involved suicidal attempts — sometimes with success — I often struggled with graphic images of death. It was a struggle beyond my control. It was as if the thoughts would spontaneously appear without any effort on my part. I hated it, but I couldn't seem to control it. I always shoved those images out of my mind and they never tempted me to take my life, but the occasional, spontaneous view of it was disgusting and I wished I could rid my mind of it.

I told my mom I was considering getting professional help. I was ready to be able to get out of my emotional rut, but had no idea how to do it. My mom agreed with me, then said, "Maybe what you need is divine intervention." I knew she was right, but how was that going to happen? I knew nothing about divine matters except that my prayers seemed to go unanswered. Even though my mom didn't have any real answers for me, somehow I felt a little better after talking with her.

On one of my occasional good days, I decided to leave work on time. I even offered to take Jo out to eat. She was excited to be able to spend some alone time together; it had been a long time. We agreed that she would meet me at dispatch at 5:00.

When I was getting ready to wrap things up and leave, my phone rang. I debated whether I should pick it up for fear of the call ruining my evening plans. For some reason, I decided to answer. It was Kyle on his cell phone. He told me that he and his wife were heading to town and wanted to drop one of Lynnette's books by. I didn't want it to get in the way of my dinner with Jo, but I was also very intrigued and anxious to read their story. When he said they weren't far, I told him to go ahead and stop by the office and we agreed to meet in the lobby within half an hour.

When Jo pulled up outside, I went out to the car and told her and the kids to come inside with me. I explained to them that Kyle and his wife were going to meet us in a few minutes.

As we stood there waiting, I was terribly nervous. I had never met Kyle's wife — I didn't even remember her name. Awkwardness is my default in social situations and this was no exception. I was greatly relieved that Jo was with me. She's not shy like I am and often covers for me in conversations.

When they arrived, I looked at Jo for reassurance. My stomach was in knots as I watched them approach the glass entry doors. Once inside, Kyle introduced his wife Lynnette, and I introduced Jocinda and the kids. Lynnette greeted all of us with a hug and words expressing her appreciation for my help that morning. Her spirit amazed me. She seemed happy and untroubled. My mind held an image of them in perpetual grief, but that wasn't what I saw at all. She and Kyle both seemed at peace with life and actually seemed happy.

Lynnette said, "We've accepted that it was Anna's ordained time to leave this earth. Nothing would have changed that." At these words, I began to question the guilt I'd had for so many years. Maybe her death had nothing to do with me. They not only didn't blame me, they saw Anna's death as destiny.

As peace settled in, so did emotions. I tried to hide my tears and my shame. Both of them were so strong and I felt so weak. It didn't seem right to let them see my tears, yet it didn't seem right to hide them either. Lynnette told me how much my letter had meant to her and she opened the book to show me the special message she'd written for me in the front of the book. I couldn't wait to read it after they left. The last thing she said was, "Anna would have loved you." What bittersweet words. I wanted to believe that, because I loved Anna too, but could she really love me? Wouldn't she think I'd failed her?

What a wonderful few minutes we all shared together that day. We barely knew each other, but our lives had intersected in tragedy and now again in healing. I was filled with joy and sorrow all at the same time, and while I was anxious to read their story, I was afraid of what it might hold.

CHAPTER 21

I began a blog on July 5, 2008. I had been reading a book titled *1,001 Ways to Market Your Books,* and one thing the author recommended was creating a popular blog. Since I didn't know how to blog, I wasn't sure how I'd ever create a "popular one." I wasn't even entirely sure what a blog was until I met Amy. She was a friend who had begun coming to our church and had blogged through the illness and death of her seven-month-old baby, Emily. Her blog, *Raising Arrows,* was the first I'd ever read.

My first blog post was a little strange. I was under the impression that every blog post had to be similar to an article for a magazine. Because Amy was a writer, and had written for a few publications, many of her posts were written like articles. I called my first post *Big Trials vs. Little Trials.* I don't think anybody read it. After all, people have to know you're blogging before they start reading your posts, and I had no idea how to let people know I was blogging. What I really wanted to say was, "Hi world! It's Lynnette!" and proceed to just chit-chat a little, but it felt a little strange doing that when I knew nobody would read it. I didn't want it to appear I was creating a world of imaginary friends. I worried somebody would stumble upon my blog, see me talking to myself and quickly run away.

Then I stumbled upon another blogger named Loni. I actually couldn't believe I found her! I had been in touch with her years before, when Anna was very little. I remembered that she'd lost one baby and had a daughter Jessica who was also born with heart problems. We had visited by email a few times back then and had been able to relate to each other. When I found her blog, I noticed right away that she had also lost her 16-year-old son since we'd been in touch. It seemed strange that each of us had lost yet another child. Heartache seemed to follow both of us very closely.

I confessed in an email, "Loni, nobody reads my blog. How did you get readers?" She offered some good advice. She sent some of her friends my way and I began to receive my first blog comments. I discovered that I *really* liked receiving comments. I no longer felt I was talking to myself (although I *was* still talking to only a few).

I met a few other women who had jumped onto the blogging bandwagon and I began to form some long-distance friendships. I continued to do mostly article-like blog posts, but one day I broke free from that, and on Oct. 23, 2008, I wrote my first real-life post called, "I Knew the Day Was Coming!" It was about the day (that day in fact) that I was given the title "Grandma." I had been in Sam's Club with

Harrison, who was just over a year old at the time and an old man who was in line behind me asked, "How old is he?"

"One"

"What's his name?"

"Harrison."

"Is he your grandson?"

I reacted by blinking and then opening my eyes wide — almost as if I'd just swallowed a jawbreaker. I probably gasped out loud too. I had just had my 40th birthday and was already struggling with feeling old. I told myself, *I must not have heard him right*. It was a bad moment … a really bad moment. With obvious disappointment and an expression of being completely offended, I said, "No! He's *my* baby." I then saw his wife look at him with an expression that said, *Good job, Harold!* (or whatever his name was).

As I walked back out to the car, where the rest of my children were waiting, I thought I would cry, but they managed to make me feel better. Abigail said, "Oh, he didn't know what he was talking about!"

Jared said, "Mom, he must have been so old that his eyes were failing him." It did help just to know they loved me enough to try to make me feel better.

I rehashed the story in a blog post and my (few) readers loved it. I got 19 comments! I didn't convert all at once to the chit-chatty style of blogging, but a couple of months later I decided to try another somewhat revealing and humorous post. It was called, *The Blessings of an Ugly Kitchen*. I was admitting that I had an ugly kitchen. I even showed pictures of it! It was very daring, I know, but it was sort of thrilling too. There was a part of me that worried people would see me as a hick (after all, I did have bb's in my woodwork, duct tape to cover gaps in missing trim, and exposed bulbs instead of light fixtures). My proud side feared misrepresenting myself, but the truth was, my kitchen was ugly (and I knew pride was sin), so I went for it! Readers liked that post, too, so I didn't regret revealing the truth. In fact, that blog post made me want to be even more transparent. It gave me a desire to reveal more of my not-so-perfect life. It became sort of a challenge. Was I brave enough to be myself?

I'll admit, I loved receiving comments telling me how funny I was. It wasn't because I craved attention (although I do think that particular character trait does exist inside of me). I believe it was because I loved knowing I was adding joy to others' lives. I think it's even more important for someone like me to share joy because I've hurt so deeply. It gives people hope to see my happiness and to know that if they are suffering, they will smile again. I love being a part of that hope.

I didn't realize how therapeutic it was to just let loose and be silly. Truthfully, I've always been kind of silly, but never so publicly! I've sung *Juke Box Hero* on my blog. I've shown stupid pictures (even of myself). I've blogged about my breakfast, my mistakes, my crooked face, my kids' random, silly videos … yet I also continued to take life seriously at times. Readers seemed to enjoy reading both types of blog posts.

My blog grew from just a few readers to more than 2,000 in just over a year. This strange journey that began, simply to promote my book, became a journey to friendship, spiritual growth, and ministry. I was selling a few books through my blog, but somewhere along the way that became secondary.

*****

I was scared to death the morning I was on my way to my first book signing. I didn't have any idea what to expect and I'll admit to feeling ridiculous. Insecure thoughts and feelings overwhelmed me. *Why would anybody want to buy my book? I'm nobody famous or important. It's going to be an uneventful, humiliating day.* Usually, when I worry about things, they turn out just fine in the end, but this wasn't one of those times. When we got to Family Christian Store at the scheduled time — 10:00 am — we realized that they didn't have any posters up as promised. In fact, nothing was ready for us!

Being uncomfortable in the first place, the current circumstance made me want to say, *Well, thank you any-way! We'll try again another time,* but Kyle was determined to make it work. I am privileged to have a husband who is in sales and is very comfortable with people. Rather than leaving me to deal with the awkward situation, he just walked up to the lady who was working and said, "Hi, I'm Kyle and this is my wife, Lynnette. She is scheduled for a book signing here this morning."

The lady looked at us as if we were from the moon and said, "I'm the only one here opening today because somebody called in sick. Can you hang on for a bit?" That was fine, but then customers started coming and she was stuck behind the cash register for quite some time. Kyle continued to chat with the lady in between customers and I wandered around the store trying to look inconspicuous. While I was in hiding, I saw a friend walk in the store. She had come to support me at my very first book signing. I was a bit humiliated when I had to tell her they had forgotten about me. When Kyle realized this lady was not going to be free anytime soon, he offered to set up the book table and get things started. She was grateful for his help and I was relieved we wouldn't be standing around feeling stupid much longer.

The book signing wasn't a complete flop, but it wasn't a great success either. In the tiny little store, people walked by us looking in the other direction and sometimes wouldn't even accept a free bookmark! If they had known how insecure I felt, surely they would have made a little more effort to show interest. We did, however, meet a few interesting people and that made the two hours worthwhile.

*****

On Jan. 16, 2008, I had my first radio interview. It was in Hutchinson, Kansas, at KWBW. I was terrified, and that is putting it mildly. I asked my blogging friends to pray for me and told them I was very much "out of my comfort zone."

We were told to be there very early in the morning. In fact, it was so early, the sun wasn't completely up yet. The place was almost deserted when we arrived. There were two men in the studio doing their morning radio show and one lady in an office who had no idea who we were and didn't offer us any help. The man who was supposed to do the interview was nowhere to be found. Obviously, we couldn't barge in on the men in the studio. The sign outside the door said, "On Air," so we just sat down and waited for somebody to acknowledge us. I was told I would be on at 7:00 am, and it was 6:50 am. I contemplated walking right back out, but Kyle wouldn't hear of it. Instead, I stood up and began to pace the little foyer.

A few minutes later, I looked at Kyle with an expression that told him I was ready to go. When he stood up, I thought he was ready too, but then one of the men who was doing the radio show walked out and said, "May I help you?" We told him why we were there and he said, "Okay, give me your book and tell me in two minutes what your story is." I couldn't believe that he thought we could pull it off. We gave him the low-down in two minutes (or less). He then said, "I'll flag you in, in just a couple of minutes. Be watching for my signal." I stood there and watched through the window until I got the signal to go in. When he called me in, I was put right in front of a huge microphone and was instructed to keep it directly in front of my face. Doing so meant that I couldn't even see the man who was interviewing me.

He then said, "Ten seconds." My heart began to pound and I couldn't breathe for a second. We were on the air.

"Today we're visiting with Lynnette Kraft. She's the author of the new book, *He Afflicted Me!*

I thought *Ugh, that's not the name of the book!* I said, "Thank you for having me" and quickly realized that my microphone wasn't on. Once the other man in the studio turned it on and everything was working, the host began to ask me questions about my losses and my book. He told the radio audience that we were residents of Hutchinson, and I had to correct him. He asked me to name my children and after I said the names of all nine, I asked, "Was that nine? Did I get them all?" I hoped it sounded funny and not like I was an idiot.

After the interview was over he said, "You can meet Lynnette at Hastings Bookstore in Hutchinson tomorrow at 9:00 am."

I said, "Well, actually it's at 2:00 pm." He then called my book, *He Afflicted Me ... in Faithfulness.* I couldn't figure out why he couldn't get the title right since he was holding the book in his hand and reading it as he spoke, but he got it wrong all but one time.

Even though it didn't go as planned, I was grateful for the

opportunity to experience something new (and considering the interviewer only had two minutes to know my story, he didn't do such a bad job either). At the book signing the following day, a lady came in who had heard me on the radio; I was surprised anybody would want to come and see me after that interview.

*****

We had several more book signings lined up and I found myself wishing I didn't have to do them. After my first experience, I hadn't gained a lot of confidence. The one I was most nervous about was set up at Barnes & Noble. It was such a big store and there were always so many people in there. I was excited, yet very anxious about it.

A few days before that book signing, my kids and I drove by the store in our huge 15-passenger van. We were often in the area because Green Acres — our favorite health food store — was in the same shopping center. As we passed, I noticed a big poster in the window that had a picture of my book and my name! It was announcing my book signing. I began to scream. "AHHHHHHHH!" I freaked out and said, "Kids, look!" We drove on, turned around and drove by it again. They were laughing at me, but they were excited too. It was my first feeling of pride over my book. I floated home in that van and had high hopes for my future as a writer.

The day for that intimidating book signing came — Feb.

21, 2008. Before I left home, I posted a blog entitled, "My Book Signing at Barnes & Noble Today — Please Pray for Me!" I had been communicating very freely with my on-line friends, and I trusted they would pray for me. I also gave the place and time in case anybody wanted to come, but I didn't think I had any local followers other than people I already knew. I was excited to report back after the day was done, and hoped I'd have positive news to share.

CHAPTER 22

While Jo and I ate dinner that night, my troubles seemed far away. Instead of focusing on myself, which had become the norm, I focused my attention on Kyle and Lynnette and the short meeting we'd just had with them. It was strange, but while neither of us knew them, somehow we both felt close to them. We were surprised at how happy they seemed to be, especially considering the losses they'd experienced. We were amazed at the peace that radiated from them. It was something I desperately wanted, but couldn't seem to attain. I was a little embarrassed that I hadn't been able to hide my emotions in front of them, and even in front of Jo.

Together we wondered about the book we'd been given. The title was intriguing, *In Faithfulness, He Afflicted Me.* I thought, *What an oxymoron. What's the meaning behind that?* We had already read the inscription together in the car.

Courtney,

How can I thank you for being there with us the morning our precious Anna went home to Jesus? As I listened back to the tape of Kyle's call to you, I marveled at your tenderness and compassion. Thank you so much.

Your letter was the perfect ending for this book. Thank you for caring enough to write it. Anna would have loved you.

With appreciation and a hugely grateful heart!

Lynnette
Psalm 119:75

I didn't really understand why she wrote those words to me. I also wondered what the scripture reference was, and hoped that it would be clear after reading her story.

I was somewhat disconnected the rest of the evening because I was so excited about reading Lynnette's book. When the time was right — when everybody had gone to bed — I found a place to settle in and dig into it. The first thing I picked up after grabbing the book was a Bible. I then got comfortable in my recliner and looked up the verse Lynnette had referenced under her name in the inscription. "I know, O Lord, that your judgments are right, and that in faithfulness you have afflicted me."

Obviously this must have had something to do with the title of her book, but I had never been able to understand Bible verses and this one was no exception. I had come across people who used scripture to support their thoughts and ideas, but I never found them to be convincing. I always made the assumption that people who read the Bible and used it to justify or validate a current issue were trained to do that. I also assumed those same people didn't understand the *real world*. I didn't have anything against them, but I did question the rationality of such thinking. Logic told me those same people could really benefit from taking some science courses to discover the scientific truth behind real-life matters.

Despite the lingering mystery of the relevance of the psalm, I found myself very curious and anxious to read her story. I read the Dedication and the Introduction. I'm not sure what I expected to see there, but I became instantly aware that this was going to be a spiritual book and God was going to be the central theme. While I expected to be bored with the religious aspect of it, there was a part of me that was looking forward to it. God had always been a sort of romantic notion in my mind. I believed in Him on some level and I had prayed on many occasions, but God was still a mystery to me. I had heard of life-changing prayers and had privately, on many occasions, prayed to receive Jesus as my Savior, but those prayers changed nothing and I'd given up the notion that they ever would.

I stayed away from churches and religious conversations. The few times I had gone to church, I hated it. I actually wanted to hear what the preacher had to say and was curious about God and his word, but nobody else seemed to be listening and the sermon didn't seem to be the reason people were there. The whole service appeared to be insincere, and that made me angry. It was more like a social gathering. I had never been comfortable in social circles and the church made me feel awkward and judged by those who were there. In that frame of mind, as a person who had distanced himself from most things spiritual, I continued to read Lynnette's book.

The prologue was torture. It recounted the morning Anna died. I hadn't expected it to begin with that morning and the emotions from November 19, 2004, came rushing back. I was hit with the realization that there was so much more to the story. I hadn't known what had taken place before the call was made; I only understood those events from my narrow perspective. One view I had never considered was Lynnette's. As she recounted what was going through her mind, my heart broke for her. I couldn't imagine Jo in the same situation. I wept as she described the moment that Anna's gaze shifted from her and Kyle to 'something else' as Lynnette sang *Jesus Loves Me* to her.

I couldn't imagine the pain they must have experienced at the hospital as they said goodbye to their precious daughter — Daddy kissing her for each of her brothers and sisters — both of them talking to her and touching her for the last time. How would it feel to walk away, leaving your child lying there in a stale hospital bed? How could a family move on after that? My pain was excruciating as I remembered my own guilt and sadness over Anna's death. I'd had my own small, personal role in this story — the untold part — and remembered my feelings of failure. I wondered, once again, how they could be "thankful" for my involvement.

As I read on, I met their firstborn, Jared. He was the one I heard Kyle talking to the morning Anna died, the one who was in the other room praying. I then met Samuel, their son who was born with no brain and only lived 13 days. I was perplexed when she described his broken body being created that way by God on purpose. Why would God create children with such problems? I guess I had always envisioned God creating the world with a set of natural laws. I assumed there was a point when he just sort of turned it all loose to operate according to those laws. I had never thought of Him actually designing each and every person for a specific purpose ... exactly like they were.

After reading about their first daughter, Abigail, I met Josiah, yet another son born with a birth defect that took his life at a mere five days old. I just couldn't believe the extent of suffering this family had endured. *Why?* I wondered what Kyle meant when he said to Lynnette the day following Josiah's birth, "God won't bring anything into our lives that He doesn't already have planned." What kind of plan could he be talking about? What sort of plan could be brought forth by repeated sorrows?

Through the tragedies, Lynnette wrote about moving forward and allowing God to heal their broken hearts. She spoke of having faith in God. I was confused as she spoke of feeling God's touch in situation after situation and of God revealing Himself over and over again. This total reliance on God was so strange to me.

What started off as foreign and odd began to feel very comfortable to me, almost as a warm embrace drawing me to it. I began to realize that this was not the same God I thought I knew and believed in. This was an entirely different God, one who was actively working and caring for people. This was the real God.

I experienced such a strange mix of emotions as I read. One minute I found myself so sad over their heartache, and the next minute I found myself amazed and inspired. I was awed over the times they found joy and peace amidst their sorrow.

Lynnette told about the way Anna had gotten her name. Once again, I shook my head in wonder over this God who was so near to them and I found myself believing in the miraculous affirmation she had received. In just a few short hours I went from believing in a world of natural occurrences and predictable rules to a world with supernatural components. I was surprised at how easily my thinking shifted. Maybe it was because I wanted to believe in something other than my own, depressing world and I began to be hopeful that I could escape it.

A part of the story that touched my heart deeply was when Lynnette talked about the days before Anna's death. Their trip to Disneyworld especially made an impact on me. It was so apparent that Anna was behaving in a manner that, in retrospect, could only have been her preparing to leave this world. I wondered how she could have known. It seemed clear that God was preparing her to leave her family and was putting everything in order for her departure.

The events of Anna's final days were further confirmation to me that God was at work. In wonder and utter amazement, I read and I cried. God began to heal me in every way as I contemplated his complete control over life and death. For whatever reason, by whatever plan, God had taken Anna home. Miraculously, I began to be freed from the guilt and sadness I felt over Anna's death. How could I have ever thought it had anything to do with me? I became overwhelmed with the feeling of being utterly powerless.

Lynnette's book was divided into two sections and I finished the first section that night. The prologue told the story of the morning of Anna's death. Section two of the book began with that same morning. I wept all over again, but this time my tears held a little bit of hope and I suspected I was going to be able to claim my own victory.

After that horrible morning was recounted, Lynnette moved on to the moments and days after Anna's death. I felt such sorrow for Jared as he said, "Goodbye, Pookie" at the hospital, and I mourned with them as they faced the days ahead. My father's heart ached for Kyle as he spoke at Anna's funeral and rejoiced with him as he did it with success. I just found myself completely overwhelmed as I considered all this family had endured.

Being exhausted (both physically and emotionally), I closed the book. I sat there feeling completely wiped out. My mind was numb and my heart was heavy, as I'd come to many realizations. I wasn't sure what I was experiencing, but I knew something was happening to me. For the first time in my life, I honestly yearned for God and I prayed. I don't remember what I prayed, I just remember how I prayed. I prayed knowing I needed God. I needed the God of the Krafts. I needed to be rescued. I needed to be healed.

*****

Because reading took so much emotional energy, I just collapsed into bed; I slept better that night than I had in quite a while. When I went to work the next morning, I still had the book on my mind. Concentrating on my job was a challenge. I kept very busy, but was glad to only have mindless data entry to do. My mind continually went back to different pieces of Lynnette's story, and it was beginning to change the way I viewed my life. I looked forward to getting home and finishing it.

The second half of the book was about Lynnette's journey through her sorrow. I couldn't believe the words she wrote in her journal and shared in her book. Many entries were full of grief and despair, yet she also shared things that made me wonder how she could have written them. In one journal entry she wrote, "We are so excited to watch God use this situation and use us. God is faithful to allow affliction in our lives to keep us close to Him." Later, when contemplating why she should have to give back three of her children, Lynnette wrote what God revealed to her while in her pantry: "Because, Lynnette, then you never would have had the opportunity to trust me. Your faith and love for me are a result of my working in your life through these sorrows. Lynnette, you have treasure in Heaven — three precious children."

I still couldn't understand all the spiritual messages, but I wanted to be as close to God as Lynnette was. I wanted Him to speak to me like He did to her. This was a new world that had never existed for me. If this family could be healed from the tremendous losses they'd experienced ... if they could grow and thrive under such horrible circumstances, surely there was hope for me! Was it possible that the God who blessed them also desired to bless me? Was it possible I could be set free from the afflictions in my life?

I finished reading her book that second evening and was absolutely enthralled with their story. In fact, I was disappointed to be done with it. I wanted more. There was a Web site listed on the book called *Growing Through Affliction,* and I logged on. I was happy to find pictures of their family. I saw pictures of Samuel and Josiah, and also Anna. The only other image I had of her was the little picture I'd carried in my wallet from her obituary for so many years. She was such a cute little girl, so full of expression. I felt I got to know them so well through the book that it was a blessing to see their pictures on my computer screen. At the same time, it was difficult to see the pictures of their children who were no longer living, especially Anna. I felt such a connection with her. I continued to look through the Web site; I just took it all in.

When I'd stood in the Dispatch Center, nervously anticipating my meeting with Kyle and Lynnette, I'd had no way of knowing how the book they were bringing to me would change my life. When we had said, "Goodbye," I was pretty sure that'd be the last time I'd ever see them. After reading the book, though, I wasn't so sure. I found myself wanting to know them better.

I had never heard anybody talk about God the way Lynnette had. I had never heard anybody so personally describe God's graces and miracles. I thought I knew God, at least a little, but Lynnette showed me that I really didn't. Through her personal encounter, she convinced me that I believed in a god without power, without compassion and without love. I believed in a god described by words and sentiments that were of my own creation. I didn't believe the God of the Bible. Lynnette's story introduced me to the God who loved her and who loved me. I had new and beautiful insight into the spirit world and wanted to be a part of it.

Again, I prayed. I felt convicted over my sin. In humility and shame, I approached God. I called out to Him as I'd never done before. I knew He was the only one who could change my messed-up world. I begged Him for revelation and forgiveness. I asked Him, "God, please show me who you are and how I can experience you. I need you."

The next evening, after everybody went to bed, I was restless. Friday nights were normally my favorite time of the week because I had a couple of days off and could effectively lose myself and escape the real world, but this Friday night was different. Nothing in my usual repertoire appealed to me. For some reason, I didn't want to watch movies or listen to music. I didn't know what to do.

I saw Lynnette's book lying on the table, and underneath it was my Bible. I picked it up and thumbed through it for a minute. I'd read most of the Bible in my college years, but it meant nothing to me then. I never understood it. There were still some bookmarks in it from nearly 15 years before, when I had done a class presentation from the book of Luke. I couldn't remember what I had presented, but I looked at the first verse I saw marked. It was Luke 6:18 and it said, "They had come to hear Him and to be healed of their diseases; and those who were troubled with unclean spirits were cured." I had a strong inclination that these marked verses were for this very moment. I read on, "Blessed are you who weep now, for you will laugh." I knew God was speaking directly to me through the words of Jesus spoken 2,000 years before. As I read the marked verses now, I found myself wanting to start at the beginning so I turned back to the first page of Luke. It was starting to make sense for the first time!

The next evening, instead of my normal activities, I

picked up the Bible again. I started at the beginning of the New Testament in Matthew. I marked many verses as I read, some that seemed significant, others that I didn't understand. Even in my confusion, it was exhilarating. I wanted to learn. I was especially struck by the words in Matthew that said, "Those who are well have no need of a physician but those who are sick. Go and learn what this means, 'I desire mercy, not sacrifice.' For I have come to call not the righteous but the sinner."

I knew I was sick and I knew I was a sinner. Jesus had called me and I had received Him. I had reached out to Him in desperation and He had welcomed me into his loving embrace.

I suddenly had a desire to go to church. I wanted to be with God's people. I wanted to learn from them and witness Him at work in their lives. I had hated church, but now I was being drawn to the very place I had always dreaded going. I was socially handicapped and the thought of facing people in this setting was frightening to me. Every fiber of my being rebelled against going, but there was something new in my spirit that needed it and wouldn't let it rest.

There weren't many churches in our small town. I was familiar with a few of them, and while there was nothing wrong with them that I knew of, I suspected God was leading me to a particular church, and that He would let me know when I'd found it. I remembered a man named Mike who was the pastor of a little church in a neighboring town, but I couldn't remember the name. I did remember where it was, so I got on the Internet and began a search.

It took me quite a while, but I eventually stumbled upon it. The only way I knew it was the right one was by the name "Pastor Mike" on the main page. He had been one of my basketball coaches and I always liked him. For years, I'd seen him around town but had only recently discovered he was a pastor. The church service started at 10:30am, and despite my reservations, I committed to going.

I normally slept until about noon on Sundays, but this Sunday I was on a mission. It was August 31, 2008, and I was going to church! I woke the kids up and announced my plan to them; they didn't say much. They had been to church with Jo on several occasions and were used to going to a Wednesday night activity at a church, so they weren't terribly surprised, but I imagine it was a little strange going with me instead of their mom. The one who was surprised was Jo. I didn't wake her up until right before we left. I'm not sure why I didn't ask her to go beforehand. I hadn't talked to her about anything that was going on in my heart. Maybe I feared what she'd think of me and I didn't want to take the chance of being let down. We'd never discussed spiritual matters and I wasn't exactly sure where she stood. When I woke her, Jo just looked at me, confused, and obviously a little upset. I apologized, but didn't take time to explain. It was all so new to me that I wasn't even sure what was happening. I was nervous about going and didn't want to be late.

As we pulled up to the church, my nerves completely took over. I had never been inside this church and didn't know what to expect. I hoped I wouldn't be let down. I dreaded the social interaction; all I really wanted was to experience God. I was grateful I had my kids to lean on. Hannah had always been fearless and sociable, and I knew I could grab her hand for comfort and support. Maybe her confidence would rub off on me.

When we went inside, several people stopped to talk to us. When I noticed people looking our way, I became self-conscious and wondered what they were thinking. I tried not to let it get to me. It was a small church with an even smaller congregation. As the pastor preached and prayed, I felt drawn in. His message was full of inspiration and I could tell he was on fire for God. His passion was contagious and I found myself wanting more. The music, the message, the entire service was an amazing experience!

As we left, people thanked us for coming and said it was "so nice" to have us visit. They weren't judgmental and they didn't pry. They were just pleasant, caring people. When I shook hands with Pastor Mike, he recognized me and I could tell he was surprised I was there. I wondered what he knew about me. Maybe he had some insight into my life I didn't know about. Regardless, he was very kind and seemed sincerely glad we had come. The car ride home was peaceful and I was overflowing with joy. I knew I had made the right decision to go and I was sure I'd go back again the next week.

I hoped Jo would want to go with me and after our short conversation that morning, I suspected she would.

After the service, we picked Jo up and went to lunch. I wasn't sure how to tell her what was going on with me. Since I didn't jump right to it, she asked me directly, "Why didn't you tell me you were going to church?"

I told her I had decided very late in the night and didn't want to bother her. I could tell her feelings were hurt. I told her some of what I had been experiencing since reading the book. She was attentive and interested in what I had to say. She and I talked about spiritual matters for the first time in our marriage.

Jo explained to me that she'd been hoping for years that I would want to go to church. She told me that she'd begged me many times to go with her and the kids, but for some reason I could only remember a couple of those times. I honestly didn't know that God was such an important part of her life. It just wasn't something we'd talked about. God had been so unimportant to me that I must have missed or ignored her desires to bring him into our marriage and our family.

Jo explained that there was a point when she decided to just keep quiet and let God work when it was the right time. I was completely lost in my own world and had missed so much of Jo's heart. She had come to know Christ as a teen, and though she had told me that before, I guess I just never understood so I didn't take her seriously. I always believed in God and even thought of myself as a Christian. I guess I just thought she was a Christian in the same way I was.

After that first Sunday, we began to go to church together week after week. Jo wasn't always able to go because she worked unusual hours, but she loved church and always attended when she could. It was a wonderful new place for our family to go and be together, and it was a dream-come-true for Jo. She had secretly hoped and waited for me to respond to Christ. She had prayed for me many times. I'm so thankful for that now.

Over the next months, I learned a lot. I immersed myself in the word and I met regularly with Pastor Mike. He became my mentor and close friend. I spent many hours in his office at the church — talking, listening, praying and growing. It felt so good to have something to focus on — something besides me and my problems. As we talked about life, Mike continually led me to the scriptures. All the answers I'd sought for so many years were right there before my eyes. If only I'd known. I'll be forever grateful for Mike's guiding hand and companionship. His deep love for Jesus was inspiring and beautiful to witness.

Life had taken a complete turn. I had been delivered! I had been rescued! I had been saved! Life didn't become simple after that, but I became focused on the right thing. While I used to think I was in control of my life, the realization that I wasn't brought me a tremendous amount of peace. I had been failing in my life, not dealing with anything well. It was a great revelation that I had a trustworthy Savior to take care of everything for me. All I had to do was go to Him for help. I understood the scripture that said, "Take my yoke upon you, learn of me ... " I found out that it wasn't that difficult to do. In fact, I enjoyed leaving my troubles at his feet and focusing my attention on learning more about him. For the first time in my entire life, I experienced sustained peace. My depression left me. My years of hopelessness and troubled emotions seemed to be gone! I'd been set free!

*****

As Christmas approached, I told Jo I wanted to get two gift baskets — one for Pastor Mike and one for the Kraft family. They had both been instrumental in drawing me to Jesus and I wanted to offer these as a small thank-you gift. Jo did a wonderful job assembling the baskets.

As the holidays approached, Jo kept reminding me that we needed to deliver the Krafts' basket. Pastor Mike's had been delivered, but the other basket sat there. I kept putting it off because I was afraid to deliver it. When Jo asked why, I didn't have a good answer. I was just nervous to make contact with them again. They didn't know I'd received Jesus as my Savior and I knew it was something I needed to tell them. I just wasn't sure how they'd feel about it, and I knew I'd struggle to say it all correctly. I was anxious to tell them that God had delivered me from the guilt I'd carried, even though they didn't know I'd ever carried any guilt about Anna's death.

Christmas came and went, and the basket didn't get delivered. I think Jo was disappointed in me for being such a coward; however, she didn't pressure me. She knew I'd been hard enough on myself. She just took the basket upstairs and set it in the corner of our bedroom. It sat there where I could see it, and every time I looked in that direction, I felt like a failure.

A couple of months later, somebody in my extended family talked to me about Lynnette's book. Quite a few of my family members had read it by that time. I wondered how the book was doing, so I got on the Internet and searched Google. I found some reviews on Amazon.com and wasn't surprised to see that reviewers were very impressed with it. I certainly understood why. I continued to click around on some other links and came across an announcement for a book signing. It showed that Lynnette would be at Barnes & Noble in Wichita on February 21. That was only three days away.

While I was searching, I also discovered that Lynnette had a blog. I actually didn't know what a blog was. I had heard of them, but hadn't ever read one. I clicked on the link and was directed to a Web site with the title, *Dancing Barefoot on Weathered Ground*. I read some posts and looked at some pictures. It was interesting learning more about Lynnette and her family. I was amazed at the spiritual insight in her writing, but was more amazed that I was able to understand it. I was learning about God and His Spirit was moving in me and teaching me so much.

I showed Lynnette's blog to Jo and mentioned the upcoming book signing. I told her that I thought I should go, talk to Lynnette and tell her everything that had transpired. Jo wholeheartedly agreed. I had missed one opportunity and was determined not to miss another. I was so grateful that God had directed me to her blog and had shown me another opportunity. I felt I'd been given a second chance to share what He'd done in my life.

I knew I'd probably be limited on time and that there would be people standing around, so I decided I'd write Lynnette a letter. I procrastinated, and by Friday evening I still hadn't taken the time to put my thoughts down on paper. It was such an overwhelming task. Where would I start? How much should I say? I decided, again, that I'd run out of time and had missed my opportunity. I told Jo, "I don't think I can go. I didn't get anything written." Determined to guide me through my fear, Jo informed me, I *would* be going with or without a letter. She was right. I had to go. God wanted me to share my testimony with Lynnette and her family.

CHAPTER 23

Kyle, who had become my biggest supporter, personal marketing manager and encouraging sidekick, went to the book signing with me. We also took Abigail, to take pictures. When we got to the door, Abigail wanted to take my picture by the big poster on the front window. When I started to walk up to it, I tripped over a doorstop. Not only did my shoe fly off, but I just about took a tumble as well. There were people walking in and I thought to myself, *I either keep smiling or I go home* — I chose to keep smiling. As they walked by with smirks on their faces, I said, "Well, now, that's a great way to start my day here!" I hoped they were laughing *with* me!

At the front of the store was a table set up with my books nicely stacked on it. Another big poster was standing next to the table. Brad, the manager, came up and offered me a coffee from their coffee shop. Coffee always has a way of easing my tension, so I decided a Caramel Macchiato would join me for the book signing. I found myself wishing all my book signings had gone so well. I almost felt important.

There was another author there that day. She had a book

that (she said) had sold 2,000 copies. I didn't know if I was supposed to be impressed by that number, but her sharing the information seemed to make her feel pretty important. She sort of reigned over me through the whole event. At one point, she pulled me over and said, "You shouldn't be giving your bookmarks out to people without stopping each one of them and telling them your story!" I explained that it wasn't my personality to force myself on people and that I was happy to give them my bookmark because it had my email and my Web site listed. She looked at me like I was insane to be giving something away for free. I decided I would ignore her advice. I could tell she was irritating people. I watched them trying to get away from her and I was not going to be pushy like she was. Call me strange, but I actually wanted people to *like* me.

So many of my friends and family came that I'm sure I looked very important to all of the outsiders. I didn't hire my friends to come, but I was thinking it wouldn't be a bad idea to do that in the future. Yes, it was definitely a good tactic. Taking pictures with people and signing books had me floating on cloud nine.

Towards the end of my time there, I noticed a man standing off in the distance with two children. I kept expecting him to walk up, but when he didn't, I turned my attention away from him. Perhaps he was waiting for somebody and just happened to be looking in my direction. People came and went and then the man appeared at my side with Kyle standing next to him. Kyle said, "Honey, remember Courtney Becker?"

I practically squealed, "Oh yes!" The name hit me like a ton of bricks. Because I'd only seen him once, I'd forgotten his face, but I would never forget his name.

I gave him a big hug and we chatted for a bit. I remember thinking what a soft-spoken and kind man he was. Courtney radiated gentleness and kindness — like a comforting cup of coffee or a nap outdoors on a perfectly beautiful day. I was so happy that he came to the book signing, but was perplexed about how he would have heard about it, so I asked him. He told me he saw it on the Internet, which puzzled me. As far as I knew, the only way he would have been able to find it was on my blog or through the Barnes & Noble Web site. *Is he reading my blog? That would be random, but I guess it is possible.* It didn't matter. I was just so glad to have him there and to be able to show kindness and Christian love to the man who offered help and encouragement to my husband the morning Anna died.

Knowing how much Anna's death had affected Courtney made me love him more. He loved our daughter through the phone, he allowed our loss to touch his heart and he grieved with us. How many people would get personally and emotionally involved in a stranger's life?

Courtney told me that Jocinda wanted to be there but had to work. I thought it was so nice that they would want to come to support me and my book. Before leaving, he handed me a note. He said he had a lot he wanted to share with us, but because he wasn't very good face-to-face, he wanted to write it down so he was sure to express it all properly. I happily took the note and could hardly wait to read it.

Just before we wrapped it up, Abigail took a picture of Courtney with Kyle and me. I knew I'd want to share it on my blog. Having Courtney and his children there created a perfect ending to an exciting day!

When we had cleaned everything up and were ready to go, I asked Brad if I could have the posters. Of course, he said "yes" since they would have just thrown them away. I didn't plan to be tacky and put them up on my wall or anything, but for some reason I just wanted to hang onto them. It was a memory that would stick with me forever.

*****

Because Courtney's first note made such an impact on my life, I expected something wonderful of the new note I pulled out of my purse. I began silently reading it on our way home, but Kyle asked me to read it out loud.

Lynnette and Kyle,

For a long time, now, I've wanted to share with you how my life has changed and how your amazing story prepared my heart for that change.

For many years, I've been among the lost, living in and of this world with very little perception of our living God. I considered myself a Christian but what that meant was very abstract. I prayed, I tried to live a moral life, but, in fact, I was stuck in a self-centered, depressed and painful existence. Though I was receiving many, many blessings despite my disobedience, I didn't recognize that, and I just survived in my own way with limited success.

One of God's blessings to me is a tender heart, and it is through this gift that I would become engaged in the life and story of your family. When God brought us together in the lobby of the Law Enforcement Center, my transformation was in its infancy. The seed of the rebirth was planted years earlier when we met on the phone in a time of tragedy.

At this point, I realized that Courtney wasn't a Christian before, although I'd assumed he was. My spirit was telling me what was coming next and I was becoming aware of deep emotions welling up. I wasn't sure I'd be able to read the rest aloud, but I continued to try.

When we left our meeting that evening with your book in hand, I was so anxious to read it. Over the next two nights, I did read it and shed many tears. I went to your Web site and enjoyed the photographs and the beautiful music. My heart was so primed for change. Though I don't fully understand how we're drawn into Jesus, one thing that I did understand in those couple of nights was that the Holy Spirit was very much real and working in your family's life. What had always been abstract became concrete and real, and I wanted to experience God in the ways that your family was.

So many things changed in me in the span of a few days.

My interests and tastes changed. My years of avoiding Bible study turned into a desire to get into the word. My old reluctance to attend church was gone and I felt drawn to join a church. In fact, I felt guided to a small church in Goessel, where an acquaintance was the pastor. I attended that Sunday and we have gone every week since. What a wonderful blessing this church has been.

I simply couldn't go on. I felt a lump in my throat so large I struggled to breathe. So instead, I covered my face with Courtney's letter and just tried to get through the overwhelming emotion I was feeling. This had become more beautiful than I ever could have expected. I had already rejoiced knowing that the 911 call had changed his career and affected his heart, but this letter revealed that Anna's death – the most painful thing we'd ever endured – had eventually led Courtney to the feet of Jesus! He would now live forever in Heaven!

My heart rejoiced as it never had before. It was full, oh so full. I looked at Kyle and Abigail, and they motioned for me to go on. Somehow I choked out the rest of the letter.

Our family has experienced joy we never knew over the past months. They joy of living a Christ-focused life is beyond awesome! We have faced many trials, and as I grow in my relationship with Jesus, lessons in accountability and pride are common, but the wonder of the growth and blessings that are given to us through the trials are exciting! I so look forward to the forever developing relationship with Christ!

I know that one of the goals of sharing your story was to bring comfort to the grieving through the glory of God. I want you to know that, at least in my case, your story has also been used by God to bring about a rebirth, another soul saved by the blood of Christ! I am so thankful that the Holy Spirit has come into my life and I am thankful for what you have done in God's service. May you be forever blessed!

I hope to one day have the chance to get to know your family more and to share more of this story. I would also love to hear about other stories that have resulted from sharing your lives.

With Love and God Bless,
Courtney

At that moment, I knew how missionaries and evangelists must have felt when they witnessed the lost receiving Christ after their preaching or counseling. However, I had one additional element that made my heart rejoice differently, perhaps even a bit more. I had a little girl who was in the presence of our Father in Heaven, and it was her departure from Earth that touched this man's heart. God used my precious Anna, and I knew she was in Heaven rejoicing over her part in Courtney's new walk with Christ. The day that he steps into eternity, I know Anna will be at the gates of Heaven ready to greet him, hug him and welcome him into his eternal home.

My spirit was full, and I couldn't have imagined his note containing anything better than what it did. We drove home praising God and were very excited to share Courtney's amazing story of redemption with everyone!

CHAPTER 24

It was the day I had promised Jo I would go to Lynnette's book signing. I was still apprehensive, especially when I realized Jo wouldn't be able to come with me. I felt slightly panicked as I visualized entering the bookstore and meeting Lynnette. I assumed Kyle would be there and hoped we'd easily become engaged in conversation and that everything I had to say would just spill out. I was so bad at striking up a conversation that I knew it was a far-fetched thought. I really did want to share my news with them, but I was scared and I still hadn't written the note that was supposed to make the visit easier.

My anxiety had actually kept me up late the night before. I tried to start writing something to the Krafts. I even tried jotting down some notes to help me sort out and organize my thoughts, but even then it didn't come. In a mere six months, my life and the lives of my wife and children had changed dramatically. I knew God had used them and their story to prepare my heart to receive Jesus and I also knew I had to let them know.

To add even more stress to my life, I was also preparing my testimony to share at church. Though Pastor Mike and I had become very close and were meeting on a regular basis, I'd never shared my whole story with him. Based on what he did know, he suspected there was more to be told and he encouraged me to share my story with the church body. The thought terrified me, but after consideration and much prayer, I knew I had to do it.

I prepared my testimony by tracing out my journey to Christ starting with my teen years. As I put it all in order, I couldn't help but rejoice as I was reminded how God had taken notice of me in each situation and had guided me down a path that would lead me to Him. All that was left for me to do was acknowledge my need for Him and receive the beautiful gift He had placed before me. This process was very beneficial in preparing me to write my letter to the Krafts. My biggest challenge was going to be condensing it.

Sleeping in that morning created quite a bit more tension and made it easier for me to want to back out. The book signing was from 2:00 to 4:00, which meant I had to get up, get the kids ready, feed them lunch, write the letter and drive the 20 miles to Wichita. I decided if I took the kids to lunch at Burger King, they could eat and then play in the play area while I attempted to write the letter. Taylor was too old to get excited about playing at Burger King, but I knew he'd do it for me. He was such a dependable kid, and he knew from hearing my conversations with Jo that I was really struggling to get this task completed.

I ate quickly, then pulled out the timeline I had been working on for church. Studying it for a bit, I started to work through the letter. I sat there for a while trying to decide where to begin. I wanted the Krafts to understand the depth of my depression so that they could see what an enormous change had taken place. I wasn't sure how much to tell them in the letter, but I wanted them to be able to rejoice over the fact that Jesus used their story — their daughter — to completely change my life. After contemplating and second-guessing myself, I decided to focus on the time since I last met them and since I had read Lynnette's book. Perhaps I could share more another time if an opportunity presented itself.

I thought about telling them how God immediately revealed my pride after crying out to Him to save me. It was just two weeks after I'd read Lynnette's book and had gone to church for the first time. I had been helping coach Taylor's fifth grade football team and was working with a group of kids on the blocking sled. For some reason, they were struggling to get it done that particular day. As I tried to motivate them, I decided I'd show them how it was done! Being up for the challenge and the opportunity to show off, I boasted that I could move that sled farther alone than a full line of them could. I hit the sled, lifted and started chopping my feet. I was using what I thought was perfect form, but the sled wouldn't move. Embarrassed, I strained harder, giving it everything I had. Ready for my effort to pay off, I expected the sled to move, but instead I heard a loud popping sound and instantly began to black out. Barely conscious, I stood up, reeling in pain. Feeling foolish, I said to myself, "I deserved that." It was a humiliating experience, but a good lesson for me to learn. Pride was something I had struggled with my whole life, and I now knew God was trying to help me overcome it.

I spent some time in the emergency room and later on the surgical floor. My injury was a ruptured Achilles tendon. I spent a miserable six weeks on crutches recovering. One of the benefits to that downtime was that God gave me time to read His word. I craved it like a starving man would food. So, while the recovery was very painful physically, it was enriching spiritually.

After reminiscing about it, I decided not to include that story in my letter. It was too long and wouldn't fit well with what I wanted to share. I found myself wanting to be careful how much I said about myself. Even though I'd become aware of my pride, I knew it would be very easy for me to try to make myself look better than I was. I didn't want to steal God's glory in any way; the only reason I'd gained the victory in the first place was because of Him.

I couldn't seem to focus as I wrote. Kids were laughing and playing and I grew frustrated. Every direction I started to go with the letter seemed to be wrong. I said a quiet prayer, asking the Holy Spirit to guide my thoughts and bring forth the words that would be just right.

I was running out of time and the fear of failure set in. I had to concentrate! Looking up from my blank page with a huge sigh and little hope of getting the letter written, I saw a family from church walking into the restaurant. Though I didn't know them well, just knowing they were from my church somehow provided me spiritual support and quieted my heart. We spoke to each other for a moment and then our children began to play together. I knew God had prompted me to write the letter, and he used the family from my church to give me a gentle reminder of his presence.

Miraculously, the words began to flow. I began to feel my testimony pour forth … out of my heart and onto the paper. I was overcome with a tremendous peace. I knew that Kyle and Lynnette needed to know the things I was sharing and I was anxious for them to read just what God had done. I wanted them to know that God used their daughter's death to save my life.

Satisfied with what I'd written, I noticed we were running very late and needed to go. I quickly removed the sheets of paper from my notebook, sealed them in an envelope and ran out the door with the kids in tow.

When we arrived at the Barnes & Noble parking lot, my anxiety returned. I was reluctant to go in, but then I thought of Kyle and Lynnette and knew they would be happy to receive my letter. I said a quick, silent prayer and asked the kids, "Should we go in?" Like they so often do, they rolled their eyes at me and said, "Let's go, already!"

They were heavy steps that led me from the parking lot to the entrance. As I approached the doors, I saw a poster announcing the book signing. We walked in and saw Kyle and Lynnette standing by a table stacked with her books. They were both engaged in conversation so I waited to speak with letter in hand. I was thinking, *I sure wish I could just get this over with,* but God had more to teach me than humility; I had to learn patience, too.

When I saw Kyle was available, I approached him. He greeted me and reached for my hand, but didn't seem to recognize me. I guess I shouldn't have expected him to, but I hoped he would so it would be less awkward. When I remembered how to introduce myself, I said, "Hey Kyle, I'm Courtney Becker." He lit up and quickly regretted not recognizing me. He had just been so preoccupied that I think I caught him off guard. We talked for a moment, then he took me over to Lynnette. He introduced me and she remembered me as well. I was so nervous, I didn't know what to say. I began to talk fast and laugh too much, which is a normal nervous reaction for me. That realization made me even more uncomfortable.

I told them I wanted to buy some books for a couple of my friends, so while Lynnette signed the books I watched their book trailer on a laptop computer. It was dramatic and sad. A bit of Kyle's voice and mine were on the trailer. I began to get emotional and worked very hard to hold back the tears.

I realized I just didn't know what to say to these amazing people. I had shared a small moment with their little girl, but it didn't feel small to me. I'd grown to love Anna and her whole family. I gave up the notion of having enough confidence to tell them what I came to tell them, and decided the letter would have to do that for me. I handed it to Lynnette and said, "I wrote some things down that I wanted to share with you. I didn't think I'd be able to say it right." She thanked me with a huge smile, which helped put me at ease. She then handed me the books, held the note up and said, "I'm looking forward to reading it. Thank you."

Taylor and Hannah had wandered over to the children's section, so after receiving the inscribed books back from Lynnette, I said "Bye" and went to retrieve them. After I walked away, I felt some relief. My only remaining fear was the thought of having to walk back by the two of them on our way out. I hoped Lynnette wouldn't start to read the note before we were gone. It would be very awkward.

When I found the kids and was helping them finalize their selections, I saw Kyle walking towards me. Feelings of anxiety struck. I thought, "Oh no. She read the note and now she wants to talk," but when he arrived, he just smiled and asked if we would stop back by before we left so we could get our picture together. What a relief that was! Abigail took a couple of pictures of Kyle, Lynnette and me, then I was gladly on my way out the door. As the kids and I got back in my truck, I let out a huge sigh of relief and thought

to myself, *I did it.* I prayed a quick, *Thank you Lord,* then we
headed back home.

*****

I wondered how my letter was received. Jo had been
wondering the same thing and called me that evening from
work to find out. I told her about our visit and said I wasn't
sure how it went. It has always been hard for me to evaluate
social situations objectively, so I truly didn't know.

After the kids went to bed, I decided to visit Lynnette's
blog to see if she had posted anything about the book
signing. I nervously read through her post and chuckled at
the way her day had started, losing her shoe on the way into
the bookstore. I read about the visitors she saw, then I read
about our visit. I realized that the letter I'd written had overwhelmed her.

Just as I'd hoped, she was rejoicing over God's work
in my life. Lynnette was excited that God had used Anna
to open my eyes and draw me to Jesus. She had posted
pieces of my letter on her blog and even said that she was
sure I wouldn't mind — I didn't mind at all. She had also
posted the picture of all of us. I rejoiced over the fact that I
actually followed through with what I had planned to do.
Most of all, I was thrilled that they now knew the impact
their lives had on me and on my family — an additional
miracle of Anna's life! I knew they would acknowledge it as
God's hand in bringing yet more joy from their pain.

*****

Just two weeks later, I was scheduled to present my testimony at church. Since I already had my timeline put together and had already delivered a sort of mini-version of my story to the Krafts, I believed my final presentation would come to me easily. I had been reading a lot of scripture, had spent a lot of time in prayer and was confident that the Holy Spirit would guide me to just the right words.

On the Saturday evening before my presentation, I still wasn't completely ready and I was slightly panicked. I couldn't find a quiet place to work at home, so I went to the Dispatch Center. I locked myself in my office with my notes, my Bible, a couple of books and a large mug of coffee. It was there that I finalized my notes and allowed God to calm my spirit.

After I was fairly confident I had documented everything I wanted to say, I rehearsed my speech. I knew I'd be nervous, which would make me talk fast, so I figured that into my estimation and decided it would take me about 45 minutes.

I got home around 2:00 am and tried to sleep, to no avail. I could not remember a time I was so nervous about a presentation! I had done countless presentations at work and talked to large groups of people many times. While it wasn't something I ever enjoyed, I'd learned to cope well … but not this time. God was stretching me and asking me to do things that were very hard for me. This wasn't business. This was a story about how God cared enough to take a desperate man and give him a new life. I wanted everything to speak to God's glory. I wanted Him to be the central figure. I wanted to please Him. Just as God had been seen so clearly in Lynnette's book, I wanted Him to shine through the story that He created in me. It was a testimony of His patience and His grace. The victory in my life was only because He had worked. I had tried numerous times to gain some sort of salvation and peace without Him, but had failed over and over again. It wasn't until I saw my need for Him that things changed. I changed. I was a depressed and lonely man who needed Jesus and He met that need as soon as I cried out to Him in sincerity. He answered my desperate cry and changed my life. It seemed so simple now.

I got up early, exhausted from the lack of sleep and took Hannah to Sunday school. Taylor and Jo would join us right before the service began. I went to Sunday school as well, but after about 15 minutes, I felt sick and went to the church library to pray. I reviewed my outline for a while, then I prayed some more. When Sunday school was over, I waited in the entryway for Jo and Taylor. I told Jo how nervous I was, and she gently hugged me and said, "It's okay, you'll do great."

When we entered the sanctuary, Pastor Mike was there. Sensing my anxiety, he took my hand and said a quiet prayer for me. That prayer was what God used to bring me overwhelming peace. As I went to sit with my family, I realized my burden had been lifted and I was ready to share what God had done in my life.

As we sang in worship, I realized just how much each song ministered to my heart. It was as if they had been picked that day just for me. The words were rich and affirming. I truly felt that God wanted me to speak that day. He wanted me to speak the words that He had put on my heart describing my long journey away from Him and ultimately my difficult but amazing journey back to Him.

I walked up to the podium with humble courage. I told the story of how everything in my life had changed just six months before. I talked about my childhood, my early experiences with the church and shared the emergence of my depression as a teenager that led to many poor choices. I spoke of the consequences of poor decisions and how one of those consequences was used by God to place me in the very town where I was now attending church. I shared my college years and my continuing depression, and then I shared about Jocinda, Taylor and Hannah and what a blessing they'd been in my life.

After I mentioned the start of my career in 911 dispatching, I struggled emotionally as I shared the call I took on November 19, 2004. It was the call God used to begin to soften my heart. It was when I first met Kyle during Anna's last moments on Earth. I described my sorrow and my sense of failure. I told about my connection to the Kraft family, the impact Lynnette's book had on me and I tried to explain what happened to me spiritually, how God gently led me to Him.

I told the story of how I was brought to the church with a new heart and a new desire for spiritual things. And I spoke of how the Holy Spirit had revealed God's truths, God's grace and God's daily miracles to me time and time again. I concluded with these words:

In bringing this story full circle, I just want to one last time express my awe at the way God brings all things together for the good to those who love Him. As a teenager, He took my failures and my sin and He delivered me to a new place where I would eventually feel very connected and safe. As a young adult, He provided me many opportunities and blessings despite my sinful and broken nature. He brought me to a wonderful woman who would lovingly accept me and tirelessly put up with me. We were blessed with beautiful children that bring us daily joy. He entrusted me with work that would one day connect me to a family through tragic loss. He laid the loss of that family on my heart so that I could later feel connected to their story. And through their story, God showed me many things about His love for me and His intimate involvement in my life. He provided that story to me at a time when I was most broken and when my heart and mind were ready to acknowledge that my ways of living only led to dead ends. I believe the Holy Spirit was truly interceding on my behalf at that moment, which led to the nearly instantaneous removal of obstacles and changed desires that would allow me to enter into a personal relationship with Jesus Christ, my Savior. The peaceful surety of forgiveness and salvation that accompanied this new relationship stirred in me the desire to worship my Lord and to grow in my understanding of Him. And this new fire is what brought me to this congregation that I can learn from and grow with. And, to me, this is Romans 8:28 in all its glorious wonder!

I was at peace. I felt the presence of the Holy Spirit. Other than receiving Jesus Christ as my Savior, sharing my testimony with my Christian brothers and sisters was the single most amazing experience of my life.

CHAPTER 25

10 Months Later ...

It was late morning on Christmas Eve day. I had just finished my bath and gotten dressed. My curly, somewhat out-of-control hair was still wet and my make-up had not yet made its way to my face. I was walking through the dining room and Abigail said, "Mom, Courtney Becker's at the door!" I absentmindedly said, "Who's Courtney Becker?" When I said his name out loud, I realized exactly who it was. I then excitedly repeated, "Courtney Becker!" I glanced over at the door, which had a long oval window, and saw Courtney, his wife and their daughter Hannah, all with big smiles on their faces. I let them in out of the cold and they handed me a huge Christmas basket. I said, "Oh, is that for us? It's beautiful!" I took it, set it on the table and began to peek inside. The basket held flavored coffee and hot cocoa, a couple of cute mugs and various snacks from Prairie Harvest (a local health food store). I proclaimed excitedly, "It's just perfect! We love coffee!" They reminded me that they knew that from my blog where I'd posted about my Starbucks habit on many occasions. I had to laugh at myself.

I was only slightly embarrassed about my *raw* look, but did wish I had had time to at least put my make-up on. I offered them a seat, but they mentioned they were on their way to see family for Christmas and were just dropping the basket off, so we just stood around the dining room table and talked. I introduced all of my kids and they mentioned that they recognized them from my blog. I was flattered that they spent time reading about our family.

Kyle was in the cottage behind our house playing his guitar, so Jared went out to get him. When he came in, we visited for a while. They didn't stay very long, but their visit produced a warm, fuzzy feeling I got every time I saw them. It's like I get spiritually star-struck every time I'm reminded of the whole miraculous story. My heart rejoiced all over again for Courtney's transformation. There were so many things I wanted to know about him and his family and his new walk with Christ. I hoped we'd have an opportunity someday to just sit down and talk.

*****

One Sunday afternoon, Kyle and the kids went to a movie and I stayed home with Harrison. While he took a nap, I watched a movie we had received from my mom and dad for Christmas. It was called *The Christmas Miracle of Jonathan Toomey,* based on a story I had read to my kids for years at Christmastime. It's about a widowed woodcarver who carves a nativity scene for a widow and her son. It's a touching story about how a little boy and his mother changed the life of the woodcarver through their interaction with him.

After it was over, I thought, *I wonder if I could write a touching little fictional story.* Immediately, my mind was flooded with the thought: *Lynnette, you have a true inspirational story that would touch the hearts of many people.* The Lord brought Courtney Becker to mind and the thought, *I could write our story! I could write our stories side by side and show how God worked in each of our family's lives without us even being aware.*

I was excited at the thought of it and couldn't stand that there wasn't anybody home to talk to! I couldn't call Kyle because he was in a movie, so I called my mom instead. I knew she'd be a good listener and give me her honest opinion. My excitement grew when she caught the vision right away. Her enthusiasm ignited the flame within me.

After we hung up, I brainstormed the idea some more and could hardly contain myself. At some point, it dawned on me. *I better make sure Courtney is willing to do this before I get my heart too set on it.* I was too scared to call him, so I did a search on-line and found an email address. I prayed fervently that God would make it clear to Courtney that he *should* do it! I knew there'd be no way of writing the story without him because I didn't know him well enough. I didn't actually know much about his side of the story at all. I also knew it'd take a lot of work on Courtney's part, and

I wasn't sure he'd have time or want to put forth that much effort. So, I sent a slightly spastic email expressing my excitement over what I felt God had impressed upon my heart. I had a definite vision, but the vision became an actual project when I got this response:

Lynnette,

I am in favor of anything that may be able to bring others the joy that we have! Jocinda and I know and encounter so many people that I wish could see life through new eyes for just a moment. I know how they can be healed, but I don't know how to engage them, how to plant that seed. The times that I have talked about Jesus outside of the church setting have been difficult and awkward (but I still hope that a seed was planted!). I have learned that a desire to be comfortable is generally opposite of what God seeks for me, so with prayer and preparation I am up for anything that you think would be useful!

I do pray that God can use Jocinda and I to reach people who need to know Him, and I have been amazed at how those prayers are answered. I will pray about this specifically and talk to Jocinda to get her perspective. If we allow God to direct us, then how can we go wrong? Perhaps we can visit later in the week and see where we are led!

Talk to you again soon!

Courtney

I took that as a "yes" and started writing my book that evening. In fact, I wrote several chapters in just a matter of days.

CHAPTER 26

I was surprised when Jo said, "Are we going to take that gift basket to the Kraft family this year?" The undelivered basket had remained in the corner of our bedroom for an entire year. I'm not sure why I didn't get rid of it. I think it was because Jo had put so much work into it that I felt guilty tearing it apart. It was a constant reminder of my cowardice. Jo didn't share in my social inhibitions and she wanted to meet the Krafts again. I had a strong desire to re-establish contact with them as well, but it was a much bigger challenge for me.

After she asked, I boldly said, "Yes, I think we should deliver it."

This year, as I thought about meeting Kyle and Lynnette again, it was different. I was still nervous — I'm not sure that my social insecurities will ever be gone — but I imagined a nice, brief meeting that never went beyond the front porch. Even though I had only talked to them a few times, I had followed Lynnette's blog for months and it seemed as if I knew her family well. I was careful to remind myself that it was a one-sided relationship. Although Jo and I knew a lot about them, they barely knew us. I wasn't necessarily seeking a close relationship, I just wanted them to know that we continued to think about them and that we were growing in Christ. Perhaps knowing that their daughter's death continued to change our lives would bring some sort of consolation.

On one of my days off, the kids and I went to pick out some new items for the basket. I was now determined more than ever to deliver it. I found myself being overly particular and the kids grew impatient with me. I nitpicked over each and every item. When I was finally satisfied with my purchases, we went back home to put the basket together. I arranged and rearranged, trying to create the perfect gift, but the basket from the previous year just wasn't going to cut it. It sagged strangely and looked odd. If I was going to deliver the basket, it was going to be just right, so off I went to purchase a new one.

Jo congratulated me on my work, then asked, "So, when are we going to deliver it?" I decided we'd go the next day — on Christmas Eve. It'd work out just right to drop by on the way to a Christmas celebration we were going to in Wellington. Jo suggested we call ahead, but I told her I didn't want it to be formal and I didn't want to make a fuss over it. The truth is, I just wanted to stop by for a minute and drop off the basket, and I secretly hoped they wouldn't be home! I would have been happy to just leave it on the porch.

The next day, as we approached their farm, I was a little disappointed when it appeared they were home, but I didn't dare say anything to Jo. I was curious if they'd recognize us. I hoped we weren't being rude just showing up unannounced. Not having a shy bone in her body, Hannah was the first one out of the car. Being like me and not enjoying awkward social situations, Taylor decided to wait in the car. I understood that all too well and didn't force the issue. As we approached the porch — basket in hand — I sighed deeply and nervously smiled at Jo. She offered back an encouraging grin.

We were greeted at the door and invited in. I hadn't planned to go inside, but found myself not knowing how to manage staying out on the porch. When we walked into the dining room, I was sure my apprehension was obvious to everyone there. Feeling self-conscious, I let Jo and Hannah do most of the talking.

All of the kids were in the room with Lynnette. I'd seen them on her blog, but had only met Abigail in person. Everyone was trying to make conversation, but there were a few moments when it was obvious — at least to me — that the situation was a little strange. As Lynnette and Jo talked, I began to relax a little.

Jared, Abigail and Cecily were all standing together, watching the unscripted scene. Silas and Harrison were drawing pictures of monsters, which they were excited to show me. Jonas was copying some Greek text out of the Bible! I thought, *What kind of child does that?* (Lynnette assured me he's not a brainiac, but rather likes to pretend he's Indiana Jones on the hunt for some lost treasure.) At some point, Jared went to get Kyle. When he came in, we shook hands and engaged in some light and easy conversation. I was glad to be in the presence of this family I'd spent so much time thinking about. There was a certain satisfaction in it. I was especially glad I had enough courage to deliver the basket.

The conversation became easy and it was fun getting to know them a little better. I'd visualized the whole scene ahead of time, and wanted and expected it to be brief. Because of that, I gently closed the conversation after about 15 minutes and led my family out the door.

We celebrated Christmas several times that weekend before I had to return to work on Monday morning. After a week of vacation, I had many voicemails and emails to sort through. As I neared the end of my list, I saw that Lynnette had sent me a couple of messages. I wondered how she'd gotten my email address. I didn't remember giving it to her.

After dealing with all of my official business and grabbing a cup of coffee, I anxiously began to read the emails from Lynnette. I smiled as I saw how her thoughts were flowing. She started with one idea in her first email, then went on to another in her second. The idea she'd settled on was that she wanted to write another book telling our stories together.

Dear Courtney,

I feel very inspired to write another book! This book would tell how God intertwined our lives together through Anna. How God brought tragedy to our lives and affected yours for eternity is still so amazing to me!

If you would permit it, I'd like to ask you a gazillion questions and peek into your private life and learn just how Anna's death affected your life. I would like to talk to your wife and have you write out or tell me actual things that happened after you took the call. Then I'd like to learn about your life moving on...

Eventually, I'd like to get to the moment when Kyle called you and learn how that made you feel and what emotions it brought back. I'd like to learn about how God tugged at your heart through those years. I'd also like to talk about the day we met face to face when I gave you my book, and then learn how God worked in your life and in your family's life after you read it. I'd like to know what emotions surfaced and what transpired after that.

I think it would be a wonderful book! God bringing two families together through tragedy — beyond their control and even completely unaware of how God was working, only to find out years later just what work God had done. I want to show the beauty in God's intervention and perfect plan.

I'm so excited about sharing our story and would love to work with you and your family on this project.

What do you think?

Your sister in Jesus,
Lynnette

I couldn't help but be excited after reading Lynnette's idea. I did want to share our story. I was still trying to figure out how to tell people I knew and loved how God had reached out to me and saved me from my sad life, so I definitely wanted to participate in whatever Lynnette had in mind. I also knew I'd better pray about it and discuss it with Jo. I needed to guard against my own desires for my life and make certain I was doing it for the right reasons. I knew that only through prayer would I be able to discern if this proposed project was from the Holy Spirit.

That evening, I showed Lynnette's email to Jo and right away she felt it was something we should be involved in. I discussed my fears and insecurities with her. Most people I knew and interacted with didn't understand what had happened to me. I wasn't trying to be private about my faith, I wasn't ashamed of it, I just didn't know how to share it without stumbling over my words. I wasn't sure I'd be able to respond appropriately if they questioned me or made fun of my faith. I hoped it was evident to those around me that I had changed, but this would be laying everything out in the open. Through a book, we would be experiencing a whole new level of vulnerability.

Would there be people important to me that wouldn't understand? Would my friends and family treat me differently?

Would there be consequences I couldn't foresee? Jo and I asked each other whether it mattered, and we both agreed that if the Holy Spirit was leading us and if God was being glorified in it, then we were doing the right thing. The world's reaction is irrelevant if it pleases God. We recalled how the Kraft family had learned to trust God through incredible difficulties. Surely, we'd be okay. God would take care of us.

Jo and I prayed together and we both felt led to proceed. I emailed Lynnette and told her we were on board, and she recommended we meet so that we could get to know each other better. Both excited and nervous, Jo and I agreed. Lynnette had already started writing her story and was anxious to begin to write ours.

CHAPTER 27

We met with Courtney and Jocinda on Saturday, January 2, 2010. The only reason I was anxious about the visit was because I had so much I wanted to talk about and wasn't sure how I'd be able to ask all my questions while still being hospitable and personable. I had wondered about so many things since I'd been in touch with Courtney. I wanted to know about him, his wife and his children, but I also had questions regarding the phone call, his conversion, his thoughts about my book and especially about his life before Christ. I wanted to know the depth of his healing.

I became so engaged in the conversation that my plans to take notes flew out the window. I was surprised by some of the things Courtney opened up about. I was also caught off guard by some of what he expressed about his heart. The effects of Anna's death were so much deeper than I'd realized.

Courtney mentioned that he was a little intimidated by us. I laughed and said, "Well, if you sit here long enough, you'll realize there is absolutely no reason to be intimidated by us!" I was honest and said, "There's one danger to getting to know us better. You're going to realize very soon that we are just regular people." After that, I set out to be as real as I'd ever been, just to set Courtney's mind and heart at ease. When people come over, it's always my goal to make them feel at home. I love when our guests go to the kitchen and help themselves! It shows me that they're comfortable. I also like when they take off their shoes and hike their feet up on our couch. I'm just so much more at ease when I can tell they are.

My friend Renee and I had met for breakfast earlier that day and she was excited as I talked to her about the book. Tears welled up in her eyes as she tenderly said, "Do you think one of God's special callings on Anna's life was to help Courtney see his need for Jesus Christ? God knew from the moment he placed Anna in your womb that someday her death — which would cause you so much pain — would bring Courtney to Jesus. He knew that Courtney's profession of faith would be another piece of your healing."

I knew there were many reasons God created Anna. She brought joy to all of us and helped us change our view and perspective on life and love. I replied, "I know! I *do* think God planned to use Anna for Courtney's sake from the very beginning. It just took time for it all to play out."

I thought it would be an encouragement for Courtney and Jocinda to hear about that conversation, but when I mentioned it, Courtney's face quickly turned bright red and he turned towards Jo. He buried his face between her shoulder and the couch and began to sob out loud. It wasn't a silent breakdown. It was painful and deep. I looked at Kyle with eyes that said, *Oh my gosh, what did I do?* I felt wretched. I thought it would comfort him to hear those words, but I felt I had crushed him with my words. Seeing a man cry — even in a movie — has always moved me to tears, so I immediately turned my head and let my own tears fall. The silence was awkward, so I gained a little composure and resumed the conversation. Courtney lifted his head and seemed to be doing better, but I just sort of talked in circles, practically unaware of what was coming out of my mouth. Kyle saved me from my ramblings by bringing up something else.

Amongst the crying and laughing, we talked … a lot! Most importantly, we had sincere fellowship as brothers and sisters in Jesus Christ. We spent six hours in our living room getting to know each other, but I still had so many questions! I decided I'd have to save some for another time.

It was incredible to realize where we'd been and where we had ended up. It also made me sad that the Beckers had never known Anna. Had she been home when Courtney and Jo had arrived, she would have been waiting by the window with Cecily, watching them get out of their car. They both would have opened the door and greeted them. But if Anna had been home that day, they wouldn't have had a reason to come.

CHAPTER 28

It was a quiet 20-minute drive from our house in Hesston to the Krafts' home near Sedgwick. Jo and I thought about how our visit with Kyle and Lynnette would unfold. Because of my tendency to get nervous, Jo left me to my thoughts. Taylor was out of town visiting an aunt, but Hannah was looking forward to making new friends!

Most of my more serious communication with Kyle and Lynnette had been done in writing, so once again I feared the face-to-face interaction. I knew I was at risk of wearing my heart on my sleeve, as usual. I also knew, beyond a shadow of a doubt, that I *would* break down at some point.

About five miles from the Krafts' home, I felt a wave of emotions pass over me. It was a mixture of my sorrow and shame combined with joy and thankfulness. It came on suddenly, and in an instant, tears welled up in my eyes. I looked away and wiped my eyes, hoping Jo hadn't noticed.

From the moment we walked in their home, Kyle and Lynnette treated us as longtime friends. They both had an obvious peace that made them easy to be around. Their home was tidy and inviting, and they had snacks and coffee set out on the coffee table for us to enjoy while we visited. It was a blessing to fellowship together and become better acquainted.

Kyle and Lynnette shared little details about Anna's life. They told us things about her personality and described the things she liked to do. I found myself wishing I had known their family when Anna was still alive. Sitting in their home where everything had taken place seemed surreal.

Lynnette and I talked about the guilt each of us had felt after Anna's death. Though I knew God had released me from that, and I knew Kyle and Lynnette didn't blame me, I realized that I hadn't fully released myself from that guilt. This became obvious when we discussed whether one of the purposes of Anna's life and death was so that I would come to know Jesus. This was something I *had* thought about many times, and it grieved me deeply that it took the death of a child for me to come to understand my own sin. While I knew Anna's life and death had been completely in God's hands, I was still confused about my own culpability in Anna's death. What if I had gotten on my knees sooner? What if my veil of pride, which had blinded me for so long, had been removed in a different way? What if I had simply been obedient to God? Would Anna still be here? No. I knew there was more to it — and it wasn't all about me — but in vulnerable situations, I continued to struggle with understanding that.

With these questions still lingering in my heart, I felt deeply sorry for whatever part I'd played in Anna's death. Sobs of remorse welled up in me, and as I hid my face behind Jo's shoulder, I hoped that Kyle and Lynnette understood my sorrow as an unstated apology from me to them. I imagine there will always be a certain sadness in my heart until the day I can meet Anna in Heaven, give her a hug and tell her that I love her … and that I'm sorry. On that day I envision her taking my hand and leading me off to meet Jesus, just like she and her mother did here on Earth.

Despite the tears we shared that day, the four of us really did have a wonderful time. We discussed a variety of topics, but our conversation always returned to how God threaded our families together behind the scenes. As we talked about their experiences and ours, it was so obvious that our two stories — our separate lives — were destined to belong together somehow. The Kraft family had a story of immense emotional pain, healing and ultimately victory in their closer relationship with Jesus. I had a story of immense emotional pain, healing and ultimately victory in a newfound relationship with Jesus. Each separate story is a beautiful reflection of a loving God, but this story, the story of two families being woven together in God's sovereignty, provides an unmistakable glimpse of a perfect God who knows all, sees all and acts with divine purpose on our behalf, even without our awareness!

On November 19, 2004, I routinely answered a call. That call began to change me, and four years later, that call transformed me. Through God's miraculous love, I was able to finally grasp who He really was. At last, the blinders were removed from my eyes and my soul was set free! In 1990, God used Kyle and Lynnette's baby to draw them to Him; 18 years later, God used their little girl to draw me to Him.

Through Anna's death, I gained eternal life. I'll be forever grateful to God for not forgetting me. I deserved to die, but He loved me enough to pull me from the dark and lonely pit I lived in and give me eternal hope. In saving me, God gave my kids a new dad and my wife a new husband. He renewed my love for my work as the director of dispatch at the 911 Center, and gave me purpose, value and overwhelming peace.

When I was down, Jesus loved me. When I was lost, Jesus loved me. When I was weak and broken, Jesus loved me. Then, when I cried out to Him, Jesus loved me again … with the truest, most sincere love that ever existed. I will always be grateful for that love because, without it, I would have no hope. My life was on a fast downward spiral, but Jesus pulled me out and rescued me. His love changed my life.

AFTERWORD

As Courtney and I began to communicate about the book, I grew very excited to learn more and more about his life and the connection that God had made without our knowledge.

One thing I discovered after I began writing was that Courtney's two children each had a piece of Anna's name. Hannah had Anna's first name right in the middle and Anna's middle name, Gabrielle, contained Taylor's middle name, Gabriel. That may not seem important to some, but I know it was divine. I had given birth to nine children and the only two names out of all 18 (first and middle) that fit into Courtney's kids' names were Anna and Gabrielle. Coincidence? I'm certain it wasn't. I fervently believe that Anna was always meant to be a part of their lives.

I also rejoiced when I asked Courtney at what point he started his career in 911 dispatching. I shouldn't have been surprised when he said "July 1998." I just opened my eyes wide, smiled and shook my head in amazement. That was the month and year of Anna's birth.

Courtney and I wrote most of this book in just two

months. It came together perfectly; however, at some point, Courtney and I both experienced debilitating pain while we wrote. For Courtney it was headaches, for me it was chronic neck, shoulder and arm pain. This slowed us down for a while and I became very discouraged. There were days I would sit down to write, and just looking at the computer screen brought pain — as though my body was telling me to stop. Through perseverance and much prayer, God helped us to complete the book. Because of that, I know God has beautiful plans for it to touch lives and that it will be another one of those things that God uses for His glory! Perhaps there is some hidden message or lesson to be learned within the pages that we aren't even aware of. That's the kind of God we serve — one who just wants us to move as He directs our way.

Anna's life was blessed, but so was her death. I know she'll be at the gates of Heaven to greet Courtney the day he enters in because God used her death to give him life. Courtney's life changed the morning he answered Kyle's phone call. How could he have known what God had in store for him? He was just doing his job when he routinely answered, "911 dispatch." Who would have known that the little detail he got wrong — Anna's name — would also be the very thing that was used to draw his heart into the conversation and make him sensitive to God's calling. I know it wasn't a mistake. I know that divine intervention was the reason … he heard Hannah.

(A Note to)

Courtney,

As I wrote this book, I got to know you and your family very well. I not only gained a brother through Anna's death, but I gained a friend. I know this book will touch the lives of those who read it because it touched mine as I wrote it. As you shared your story with me and I shared it here in this book, I rejoiced! I was reminded that we serve an amazing God! He doesn't need us to plan or predict things, He just wants us to follow His lead and answer His call for our life.

I can't tell you how grateful I am that you chose to share your story of redemption with us. I suppose you could have just kept it a secret, but then we would have missed out on one of the biggest blessings of our lives. This story needed to be told because it's one that will help others realize that, just because they don't see God at work, doesn't mean He's not. Nothing will thwart His plans.

God had you in mind the day He gave He gave Anna to Kyle and me, and I'm glad He did. We had her to love for six years on Earth and forever in Heaven and you, my friend, will now be there to spend eternity with us. God worked out many beautiful things through Anna's death, but even if it would have been for your benefit alone, your eternity in Heaven was worth her early departure and even worth my broken heart.

Lynnette